THE
NEW TALENT
PLAYBOOK

THE
NEW TALENT
PLAYBOOK

The Ultimate Guide for Building your Dream Team

ROB LEVIN

CERTIFIED

WRITTEN
BY HUMAN

PRAISE FOR THE NEW TALENT PLAYBOOK

The New Talent Playbook is a breath of fresh air for leaders who know people are the heart of every business. Rob Levin offers a people-first guide to building cultures where top talent wants to stay and grow. This isn't just about hiring—it's about creating a future of work where teams thrive. And that's a future worth creating.

Ann Sheu - Founder & CEO, Mpowered Journey

If you've ever wondered how to assemble your dream team, this book is your blueprint. Rob Levin blends inspiring stories with practical advice to help you bring out the best in every team member. Whether you're a seasoned leader or just starting out, this is the go-to guide for building a powerhouse team.

Daniel T. Donnelly - Serial Entrepreneur & Principal, Donnelly Bldg LLC

Elegant in its simplicity; powerful in execution. The New Talent Playbook should be required reading for any entrepreneur seeking robust growth of the company's top and bottom line.

Jack Daly - Serial Entrepreneur, CEO Coach, and Best-Selling Author

Finally, a better way to build your dream team, without the drama. Entrepreneurs and leaders, you already know: human capital is the real currency. But finding and holding on to top talent? Brutally hard. Rob Levin makes it easier-without compromising what matters most. A must-read for anyone serious about building remarkable teams.

John Jantsch - Author of Duct Tape Marketing

The New Talent Playbook is a survival guide for leaders navigating today's toughest talent markets. Rob Levin offers a clear and practical roadmap to build the culture, systems, and teams you need to thrive. If you're serious about building your dream team, this is the playbook you've been waiting for.

Larry Levine - Co-Founder of Selling from the Heart, Author of Selling from the Heart and Selling in a Post-Trust World

The New Talent Playbook offers a practical framework for building culture, leveraging remote and offshore talent, and navigating today's fast-changing landscape. It's a timely and useful tool for any CEO who wants a team that fuels growth instead of draining energy.

Mark Taylor - Master Chair, Vistage NYC

The New Talent Playbook is a timely and practical guide for leaders navigating today's shifting talent landscape. Rob Levin challenges leaders to rethink, reframe, and reshape how they attract, engage, and retain their people, offering clear strategies that inspire immediate action. This book is both insightful and indispensable for any leader committed to building enduring organizations.

Nelson Tepfer - Founder & CEO, ProCFO Partners

As a CEO coach and multi-time founder, I've seen leaders underestimate the talent challenge. The New Talent Playbook provides clear strategies to attract, retain, and leverage top talent using remote, offshore, and AI-driven solutions. Rob Levin gives CEOs the edge they need to build unstoppable teams and scale with confidence.

Nick Herinckx - Founder & CEO Coach, Bluefield

If you screw up talent, you're toast. The rules of hiring and keeping great people have completely changed, and The New Talent Playbook gives you the roadmap to get it right.

Norm Brodsky - Serial Entrepreneur

The New Talent Playbook is a must-read for entrepreneurs who want to build businesses that thrive without consuming their lives. Rob Levin delivers a practical roadmap to attract, retain, and leverage world-class talent so entrepreneurs can scale with confidence and focus on what matters most. If you want more growth, more freedom, and more joy in running your business, this book shows you the way.

Philip Pfeifer - Certified EOS Implementer

Entrepreneurs and leaders, you already know: human capital is the real currency. But finding and holding on to top talent? Brutally hard. Rob Levin makes it easier-without compromising what matters most. A must-read for anyone serious about building remarkable teams.

Rammy Harwood - CEO, The Corporate Source

The New Talent Playbook is the wake-up call every business owner needs. Rob Levin shows you exactly how to win the talent game by building a culture people love, keeping your top performers, and tapping into global talent and AI to scale faster than you thought possible. If you're serious about growth, this is the playbook.

Rob Dube - Author of Shine: How Driven People Can Live a Life of Exceptional Success and Profound Purpose

Rob Levin has long been a CEO's best friend, guiding leaders to deliver results. The New Talent Playbook shows exactly how to build and lead teams the way the talent game must be played today.

Scott Gerber - Chief Executive, Community.co

What I like about The New Talent Playbook is how straightforward and useful it is. Rob has a gift for turning today's talent challenges into opportunities you can act on right away. This book will help you build the team you've always wanted. I highly recommend it.

Theresa Caragol - CEO & Founder, AchieveUnite Inc.

DEDICATION

This book is dedicated to the entrepreneurs and business owners who build, run, and grow something meaningful—whether starting from a dream or taking something great to new heights—and to the enormous impact you make on your teams, your customers, and the world.

CONTENTS

Forewords *15*

1. What You Need to Succeed Today 19
2. We are in a Talent Crisis 31
3. Building a Culture by Design 43
4. Retaining Today's Top Talent 57
5. The New Way to Attract Great Talent 69
6. Expanding Your Talent Pool: The Remote Advantage 77
7. Why Offshore Talent Is No Longer Optional for Most Small and Midsize Businesses 89
8. How AI and Automation Will Help You Mitigate the Talent Crisis 103

Conclusion: Building Your Dream Today *111*
Appendix A: Why Every Business Owner Must Have An Assistant *115*
Appendix B: How WBN Helps Companies Running EOS *129*
Appendix C: WBN's Responses to Talent Provider Vetting Questions *133*
Appendix D: Additional Resources *137*
WorkBetterNow *139*
Acknowledgements *141*
Endnotes *145*

FOREWORDS

For decades, I've worked with small and midsize business owners and CEOs around the world, helping them scale their companies and build lasting success. Before that, I personally grew six startups into national players across the U.S. I share this not to boast, but to underscore this: I know this business segment—and I know Rob Levin.

I've known Rob for over twenty years as a business owner, thought leader, and client. With The New Talent Playbook, he brings to the surface what so many business leaders are struggling with—and delivers the practical tools and mindset shifts needed to win in today's talent landscape.

Everywhere I go, across industries and geographies, I hear the same thing: "Our biggest challenge is finding good people." Here's the reality: that challenge isn't going away. In fact, it's only getting tougher. That's why this book couldn't be more timely—or more important.

Rob doesn't just call out the problem—he gives us the playbook to solve it. He explains, with clarity and precision, how to build a culture that attracts and retains great talent, how to compete in a shrinking labor pool, and how to build teams that actually help you grow instead of holding you back.

Coming out of the pandemic, many business owners discovered the power of remote work—how it could reduce overhead and open up access to talent beyond local borders. Rob's company, WorkBetterNow, is fully remote (with most of its team located throughout Latin America) and scaling at an impressive pace. He shows how you can embrace remote, nearshore, and offshore talent in a way that's simple, strategic, and incredibly effective.

But that's just part of the equation. Rob dives deep into how technologies like AI and automation can help you better leverage your existing team—freeing up time, eliminating friction, and driving real productivity. And here's the kicker: the combination of AI with offshore and nearshore talent is quickly becoming a must-have for businesses that want to stay competitive. It's no longer a "maybe someday"—it's a strategic necessity today.

Rob even covers one of my favorite topics: leveraging assistants. But he goes beyond the traditional executive assistant model and redefines what leverage really looks like—showing how you and your team can stay focused on high-impact work and not get bogged down in tasks that belong elsewhere.

If you're looking for a competitive advantage in a world where talent is hard to find and harder to keep, The New Talent Playbook is your guide. Rob's done the hard work—now it's up to us to implement.

Bravo, Rob.

Jack Daly - CEO Coach, World-Renowned Speaker,
and Bestselling Author

I've built, run, and sold a lot of companies in my life. Some successful, some not so much. And I'll tell you one thing straight: the single most important factor in whether a business thrives or fails isn't the product, the marketing, or even the sales. It's the people and the culture you build around them.

Culture is what makes or breaks a company. When employees feel like they're part of something, when they buy into the values, they stick around. They work harder. They treat customers better. And customers notice. That's how you build a business that lasts. Without culture, you're just spinning your wheels, no matter how clever your idea is.

Over the decades, I've watched the world of business change dramatically. The old way of managing people—command-and-control, keep them chained to a desk, don't worry too much about their growth or their lives—just doesn't work anymore. Today's employees expect more. They want flexibility. They want purpose. They won't stay in one place just because you're paying them well. If you run your company the way you did 10 or 15 years ago, you're not going to attract or keep the talent you need to attain your goals.

That's where this book comes in. Rob Levin has written a playbook for today's business reality. It lays out what it really takes to attract, retain, and lead great people in this environment. It's not theory. It's not fluff. It's practical, proven, and grounded in real-world experience.

I've known Rob for more than 20 years. I've seen him when his businesses were interesting but not all that successful. And I've seen him now, with WorkBetterNow, a company that's thriving. One of the reasons for that success is that Rob has built it differently. Sure, part of the model is about giving companies access to great offshore talent at a reasonable cost—but that's not the whole story. What really sets it apart is how he's combined that with culture, loyalty, and smart leadership. That's what makes the company work.

And that's exactly what this book is about. If you're an entrepreneur or business owner, you can't afford to ignore it. You can get a lot of things wrong in business and still muddle through. But if you screw up talent, you're toast. This book gives you the roadmap to get it right.

Ignore it at your peril.

Norm Brodsky – Serial Entrepreneur

CHAPTER 1

What You Need to Succeed Today

---

*"Your life does not get better by chance,
it gets better by change."*
– Jim Rohn

It's challenging to run a business—and will only become more challenging in the years ahead.

Why? Because the pace of change in business is faster than ever, and it's accelerating. This isn't just a passing trend—it's a fundamental shift that business leaders have been talking about for years.

I met Gil Maurer back in 2008. Gil was a Director and the Chief Operating Officer of Hearst from 1990 to 1998, and a legendary executive in the media world. Over breakfast in the Hearst Tower in New York City, Gil explained that the pace of change in business is continually increasing. "The key to success in business," he said, "is the ability to harness that change."

Gil passed away in 2025, but his message is more relevant now than ever.

While the pace of change has certainly increased since 2008, it accelerated *drastically* during the pandemic and hasn't let up. Many business owners subconsciously feel this increase in pace, but don't really understand the power and significance of it, much less what needs to be done about it.

As a business owner, you need people who can help you keep up with the rapid evolution of change in your industry, adapt to new challenges, and drive growth.

Take AI, for example. You need people at all levels who understand the power of AI for your business and who can integrate it into your company. And it's not just AI that's changing the business landscape. Marketing is changing all the time. Customer expectations have changed and *continue* to change.

One powerful example of this is what I call the "Amazon effect." Virtually everyone is now an Amazon customer and has grown accustomed to the ease of doing everything—buying, returning, checking order status—quickly and seamlessly. Whether you're selling B2C or B2B, you're still selling to people who now hope for that same Amazon-level convenience from every interaction.

The HR side of business is rapidly evolving, too, as employees expect much more from their career experiences than ever before. Can you imagine suggesting nomadic, work-from-home arrangements to your grandparents or even your parents' generation? Or replacing annual performance reviews with continuous feedback and real-time encouragement?

Consider how fast change is accelerating:

- Landline telephones took 75 years to reach mass adoption.
- Personal computers took 20 years.
- Smartphones were everywhere in under five years.
- And AI? Over 100 million people were using ChatGPT within just two months of its launch.

That's the pace of the world we're now operating in.

As a business, if you can't keep up, you will be left behind.

Yet, to keep up, you need *time* to think about how your company needs to evolve, and you need a team of people around you who are not only open to continuous change, but who are capable of incorporating new technology, systems, and talents as the world evolves. Change drives the need to add new capabilities to your company. In short, you need a team that sees change as an opportunity, eagerly upskills when faced with new tools, and can help you deal with change as it happens, knowing that it's going to happen faster, and faster, and faster.

"Good enough" talent isn't going to cut it. You need people who not only know how to address these changes but who also have an ownership mentality to drive change in your business.

It's always been challenging to find the right people to help your business grow and thrive, but what lies ahead is even tougher than what you've experienced so far. It's shaping up to be a competition for good people that will ultimately be just as intense—and perhaps even more intense—than the competition for customers.

Business owners who don't face this reality risk seeing their companies struggle due to a lack of talent. By "talent," I mean the right people—those who are proactive, adaptable, and aligned with your mission. The kind of team members who treat your business like it's their own. Business failure is an extreme scenario, of course, but the more common reality is being frustrated with your talent and needing to "settle" when your choices for talent are hardly ideal.

Let me tell you now: You don't need to settle. You can build a dream team around you—a team of talented, adaptable, and highly skilled individuals who can keep up with the pace of change and help you thrive.

The wisdom to do that doesn't exist in the usual places. Much of what gets covered in traditional business books—and almost all of what you hear about talent, business norms, and trends in the mainstream media—is based on what's happening in and around large companies and major multinationals. By and large, it doesn't apply to you, your business realities, or your needs.

This book is different.

What This Book Offers You

In the pages ahead, I will give you The New Talent Playbook—information, tools, and tactics specifically selected to help small and midsize business owners rapidly level up their talent. It's material you can take advantage of right away, with tactics I am confident will deliver results for you.

How can I be so sure this book will help you? Let me share my story. I've spent my entire professional career—over 30 years now—working with small and midsize businesses and their owners. Initially, I helped these firms in my role as an accountant. Then, I ran several small businesses as a CFO, COO, and CEO before ultimately starting my own business in 2003. Thanks to the unique nature of that business, the New York Enterprise Report (NYER), I brought top experts to over 100,000 business owners and leaders, and had a front-row seat to what makes businesses successful.

As you might imagine, the breadth and depth of that network allowed me to see and hear things that weren't covered in the mainstream business press. I saw companies struggle and fail—including my own—as well as companies achieve amazing exits. I got to see the differences between the best and the rest. I've coached dozens of business owners formally and informally, in addition to having my own companies, and through that work, developed the ability to spot business opportunities and trends within the small and midsize business world.

For example, for the last ten years, I've been tracking a talent shortage. Around 2014, I read an article about how the U.S.

population was aging and there would be many more people leaving the workforce than entering it. I could see how the competition for talent was intensifying, and how demographic projections and changing work habits would reshape the talent landscape.

Those insights, among others, were a major part of the timing and decision to launch my present firm, WorkBetterNow (WBN). I could see the growing talent shortages, how they were uniquely impacting small to midsize businesses, and how larger companies had been tapping into offshore talent for years to address this very challenge. I realized that a similar solution in offshore talent working remotely could be a game-changer for small and midsize businesses, too.

With everything I'd learned over the years—and taking into account the mistakes I'd made along the way—my team and I at WBN created a blueprint for unlocking success by putting talent at the forefront.

When I was running NYER in the early 2000s, I thought I had a good team in place. Our focus was on growing the business and scaling, which I was able to do to a respectable level. I thought that with a great product (which we had), I could just work harder to make the business a success. But day in and day out, I found myself being pulled into different parts of the business, rather than focusing on the seismic changes that were going on (such as the shifting of advertising dollars from print to digital). At the time, I blamed my own tendencies toward micromanagement, but assigning that blame to myself didn't change the fact that I was constantly doing all kinds of work I shouldn't have been doing. *This was the culture that I created.*

I learned and grew. Then, in 2018, when Andrew Cohen and I started WBN, I could put my biggest lessons into practice.

We chose to shape our company by focusing on getting the right people into the right roles. Every hire needed to count. We wanted people with great skills and a great attitude—almost with an owner's mentality—to be the beating heart of our business. We knew we had a great concept to bring to the market—connecting North American companies with high-quality remote talent in Central and South America—but we also knew that our ability to succeed depended on how well the people we hired could deliver on our vision.

So, did focusing on the people first make a difference?

Yes. Yes, it did. In our first year of eligibility in 2024, we debuted as #114 on the Inc. 5000 list of fastest-growing companies.[1] Our three-year growth rate was 2,936%, and I'm happy to report that number isn't the result of my own round-the-clock Herculean efforts. Instead, there's a team in place that executes and makes that pace of growth an ongoing reality while I travel, speak, consult, and make time for my family and hobbies.

The level of freedom and success that I've achieved with this model is something you can experience, too.

This isn't to say we don't make mistakes or have issues—we do. But what my partner Andrew and I now realize is that most significant issues come down to people issues.

See, great people push you to be greater, rather than you pushing them. You want people who will figure out solutions to problems on their own instead of coming to you all of the time. As the owner, your job is about setting the vision for the company and creating a rewarding experience for your people.

You Win When You Make Talent Your True Priority and North Star

One key element woven into each part of this book is the need to make talent your priority.

I know from experience that there's a tendency to believe your industry or business is different. However, when it comes to the talent part of things across small and midsize businesses, it's not different. Everyone is fighting a similar fight. Talent is a constant and ubiquitous challenge, and those who get it right will outperform those who don't have it.

In small and midsize businesses, *every seat and every player counts*. It doesn't matter if you're in construction or boutique professional services, B2B or B2C, health or fintech. No business can afford to have disengaged staff members putting in the bare minimum. No small or midsize business can afford a toxic, unproductive culture with high drama and turnover, or even one that suffers from "Well, it is good enough." Everyone needs to be aligned, engaged, and performing for your company to achieve its potential.

Everything goes back to the talent and the company's culture. The culture you create will determine not only who joins your company, but also who stays, who leaves, and how much effort they put in while they're there. Yet most business owners get no training or coaching on creating the culture they want. No one has connected the dots between the talent crisis, culture, recruitment, retention, and success in a way that is useful and relevant—until now. This book will allow you to make the right connections and translate them into actions that will help your business thrive.

And thriving—not just surviving—is very much the goal. The most successful business owners know that great talent isn't an expense. It's a calculated investment. When you get it right, it unlocks the full potential of your organization. Fully engaged, highly motivated, and extremely competent people, all working to achieve your vision for your organization, can achieve milestones, stretch goals, and even the most audacious "reaches" for your company, setting you up for success in the near term and for years to come.

Ignore "The People Part" at Your Peril

It's tempting to think a great product or business model will make the biggest difference for you. However, the reality is that without a strong team to execute on your vision, the best ideas and companies struggle or fail. WBN is a great example of this. We created a terrific business model, but we couldn't succeed without a great team.

So right now, as the pace of business continues to accelerate, it's crucial to understand why talent is the lifeblood of your organization—and how to not only attract and retain the best, but also how to leverage offshore talent as a strategic advantage. We'll also look at how using AI and automation can help you keep up with rapid changes and maximize your team's capabilities.

By the time you finish reading the chapters ahead, you'll understand the steps to take to beat the odds. Finding and keeping great talent today is challenging, but it's not impossible. You can turn the quality of your talent into your company's unique competitive advantage—an advantage that will help you achieve your goals and fulfill your dreams.

By replicating the talent-first approach we spell out here in *The New Talent Playbook*, you can help your company rise to today's market challenges and navigate the pace of change successfully.

Your original dreams and vision for your business—the one where you get to focus on the most important, impactful, and enjoyable tasks while your Dream Team takes care of the rest—is entirely possible once you start taking action. To help you do that, I have created a free companion workbook designed to help you put the strategies in this book into practice. You'll find prompts and exercises to build your Dream Team Action Plan—starting right where you are, with the resources that you already have. You'll find the link in Appendix D at the end of the book.

But before you can get there, you need to understand that without the right people, you can't keep up with change, much less get ahead of it. That's way more than a challenge—it's a crisis. In the next chapter, we'll take a closer look at what this crisis really is, why it's so different for small and midsize businesses (SMBs), and what it means for you.

CHAPTER 2

We are in a Talent Crisis

"All problems become smaller when you confront
them instead of dodging them."
– William F. Halsey

You already know it's hard to find good people. Yet, most business owners seem to think this is a localized problem in their field or a temporary situation. Nothing could be further from the truth, and this false belief could be what's keeping you from actually being able to have the talent you need.

In this chapter, we will take a very direct look at the talent crisis facing small and midsize businesses. I will use data to drive home the size and scope of this crisis, which I'm sharing to help you connect the dots between the headlines you see on the news and your company's hiring challenges. By the end, you will better understand the reality you face and be able to evolve your approach to talent management successfully.

Big Companies and Small to Midsize Businesses Exist in Different Realities

If you get your information from mainstream news sources, you hear a specific set of narratives around employment and talent availability. Here's how the stories go...

During the pandemic years, talent had an advantage over business. People could ask for higher salaries and get them because so many people were stepping out of the workforce or quitting jobs in trends like the so-called "Great Resignation" movement. Now, things are back open, the stimulus has dried up, the economy is a bit softer, layoffs are back, and employers are regaining the upper hand in the labor markets.

However—and this is incredibly important to understand—these stories represent the broad strokes of what's going on at large corporations and major multinationals. Those types of organizations ebb and flow depending on macroeconomic trends. They hire by the thousands, and they do layoffs by the thousands. It's a very, very different world from where small and midsize businesses live.

In larger organizations, success often means navigating office politics, producing reports, and covering yourself in a bureaucracy-heavy environment. In a small or midsize business, it's a different game. You need people who can pivot quickly, wear multiple hats, and take ownership like a business owner does.

This is why mass layoffs at big corporations don't necessarily mean a surge of great talent for small to midsize businesses. The experience and mentality that work well in a large company don't always translate to the entrepreneurial, versatile, and driven talent you need to grow and thrive.

For small and midsize businesses, every seat counts. You work hard for each good hire and hang onto them as long as possible because, despite the headlines claiming the labor market is "softening," it's never been harder for smaller companies to get great talent. I'm not saying that to be dramatic—it's the cold, hard reality of the facts on the ground and where our future is heading.

The Perfect Storm - Why the Talent Crisis is Hitting Small and Midsize Businesses Hard

In March 2010, you had some 5.7 unemployed available workers for each open position. Fifteen years later, in March 2025, there was just 1 unemployed person per job opening, according to the U.S. Bureau of Labor Statistics.[2] Now, you can argue that back in 2010, we were coming out of a recession, and our present "soft landing" is a different situation. Fine. We've still moved from having nearly six people available for each advertised role to not even being able to come up with a 1:1 match between vacancies and people available.[3]

While you might be thinking, "Hey Rob, I typically hire people who are currently working, so the number of unemployed people seeking jobs doesn't mean much to me." It is important to keep in mind that this imbalance cascades throughout the workforce. It boils down to the fact that the labor market is tight, especially for great talent.

That assumes, of course, that any talent available has the skills needed to do the work that you need. You know that simply isn't true. So the talent that is in demand—competent, qualified people with good attitudes—has never been in higher demand, from the most basic entry-level positions all the way up to the C-Suite.

Talent is also exiting the workplace. Like other highly developed regions, the U.S. has an aging workforce. Extended life and health spans mean we have the potential to have 5 generations in the workplace at one time, and those generations aren't equally sized. Baby Boomers, the largest cohort of workers, are retiring at a rate of 10,000+ *per day*. Gen X, coming up behind them, isn't retiring yet, but they're thinking about it as the leading edge of that cohort enters their 60s.[4]

Behind them, the Millennial and Gen Z cohorts are increasing their presence in the workplace, but there are fewer of them to go around. Birth rates nationally continue to decline, and legal immigration fills just 1/7th of the gap between those exiting the workforce and those entering it.

The talent coming in now has a very different set of attitudes and behaviors from previous generations. While there are many exceptions, working your way up, paying your dues, being loyal to one company, elbow grease, and putting your nose to the grindstone… These are not core characteristics of Millennial and Gen Z workers.

GENERATIONAL DIFFERENCES IN THE WORKPLACE

TRADITIONALISTS BORN: 1925 — 1945

Dependable | Straightforward | Tactful | Loyal

BABY BOOMERS BORN: 1946 — 1964

Optimistic | Competitive | Workaholic | Team-Oriented

GENERATION X BORN: 1965 — 1980

Flexible | Informal | Skeptical | Independent

MILLENNIALS BORN: 1981 — 2000

Competitive | Civic and Open-Minded | Achievement-Oriented

GENERATION Z BORN: 2001 — 2020

Global | Entrepreneurial | Progressive | Less Focused

(Source: https://momenta.vc/insights/gen_z_enters_the_workforce)

Now, I'm generalizing broadly, and I know there are exceptions to every stereotype out there. Yet 30% of people between 25 and 34 are willing to report that they're doing the bare minimum at work,[5] and some 45% of hiring managers have declared that poor work habits make Gen Z practically unemployable and hands-down "the worst" to manage.[6] Throw in notorious trends such as "quiet quitting,"[7] and you've got a nightmare scenario for SMBs where every employee counts, and you need everyone to be fully engaged.

And that's still not all…

Increasing Wage Expectations

Even those workers who freely admit they're doing the bare minimum still expect to be paid competitive and generous salaries. As of March 2024, according to the Federal Reserve Bank of New York's Consumer Expectations survey, the lowest average salary a worker in the U.S. would be willing to accept for a new job was a record-high $81,822.[8] That's a markedly higher jump even from the 2023 numbers, which researchers say is driven largely by demands from younger workers.

This earnings mindset is the same mindset that craves fast advancement up the career ladder, with rapid pay bumps to match their rapid promotions. Small wonder that some 42% of workers say they're dissatisfied with their present wage.

Talent Scarcity

As if this wasn't enough, advertised roles can remain unfilled for months, and time spent interviewing multiple unsuitable candidates can make managers and owners alike fall behind on other important operational tasks. Worse, since the decision to go through with a hire is often made long after a serious need has been identified, small and midsize businesses intensely feel the pain of being short-handed.

And remember, it's not just about filling a seat. It's about filling a seat with someone who has the skills, mindset, and adaptability to perform at a high level. The gap between open positions and qualified talent means many organizations end up settling for "good enough" hires—people who may keep the lights on but can't push the company forward. Over time, these compromises drag on growth and erode competitiveness.

HR Compliance and Legal Complexity

On top of all this, the government doesn't make it any easier. Companies of every size face new employment laws on the federal, state, and local levels on a regular basis. These new laws are being passed with greater frequency than ever before and cannot be ignored, notes Andrew W. Singer, Managing Partner and Chair of Employment Law Practice Group, Tannenbaum Helpern Syracuse & Hirschtritt LLP.

In addition to learning and understanding how to comply with these new laws, companies must engage in new and evolving best HR practices. This is why, for many small and midsize businesses, Singer feels it is critical to make sure you now have professionally trained internal or external HR assistance and a good business-minded employment lawyer on speed dial.

Combine everything, and you have a recipe for a company fighting an uphill battle to succeed. There are not enough people to fill open roles. There are even fewer *qualified* people available. You've got low engagement, high expectations, and the risk that as you struggle to hire and right-size your business, you'll run afoul of some new law or compliance mandate.

As a result, you're less productive as an organization than you could be. Your existing staff is frustrated and overworked. Customers don't get the best from you, goals go unmet, and all the while, operational costs keep rising and rising and rising...

In a nutshell, this is why I don't view today's talent situation as "an issue" or "a challenge" for small to midsize businesses. It's a straight-up crisis.

Is Your Company Prepared?

Now, I've loaded you up with a lot of information all at once, and perhaps information that you hadn't seen compiled all in one place or hadn't been willing to look into before. So, let's take a moment to sit with the knowledge you've gained and explore how it manifests itself in your day-to-day reality.

- Do you have open positions that you're struggling to fill?

- What key tasks or customer experiences suffer because you're understaffed?

- Are there any members of your team you'd like to let go of but don't feel you could easily replace?

- In the last few years, have you accepted any candidates into your organization you knew weren't the best fit simply because they were available when you needed them? What's been the impact of those decisions?

- Do you (or others) spend time each week "covering" for under-skilled or overworked employees?

- What tasks would you immediately remove from your plate if you could trust someone in your organization to take them on? What impact would it have to free up your calendar or bandwidth in this way?

Where We Go from Here

As you can see, the struggle to find great talent is very real. For small and midsize businesses, it's not the same as what gets put on the nightly news. It's a whole other level of serious crisis.

So, where do we go from here? The tactics you've been using so far—that most companies have been using, in fact—are not suited for the present realities. You need a new approach to help you rise to the occasion and build a talent advantage for yourself, even in today's tough talent market.

In the chapters ahead, I will share a different approach with you—one that gets results in the form of high-functioning workers to staff you up and help you succeed. This will absolutely be something you can implement on your own, in any type of market niche, or implement with the help of my team if you'd like to move even faster.

You're going to learn:

- Chapter 3: Why "culture by design" and your employer brand can give you an edge in hiring today, so that the best naturally want to come work for you

- Chapter 4: How to keep top talent from walking out the door—and why it's about more than just money

- Chapter 5: What to change so you can recruit in a way that's less painful and gives you a better, more loyal, and more engaged team

- Chapter 6: How remote talent expands your candidate pool

- Chapter 7: Why expanding from remote to offshore is easier than ever and a must for the very near future (complete with all the key considerations you'll want to take into account before you offshore anything)

- Chapter 8: How AI and automation are transforming the way work gets done

- Conclusion: How to become resilient as an employer in the face of the world's ongoing talent challenges so that you always have the people you need to achieve your biggest and most important business goals

You'll also find a special appendix of additional resources at the back of this book. There, you will see why every business owner must have an assistant (and why this kind of role is ideal for trialing offshore talent acquisition models for your firm).

Let's dive in!

CHAPTER 3

Building a Culture by Design

"Culture eats strategy for breakfast."
– Peter Drucker

It can be hard to make culture a priority. You have so many other things to take care of, worry about, and deal with on a daily basis that culture can seem like an extra luxury. So, you leave dealing with culture issues at the bottom of the to-do list, day after day and week after week, until they fall by the wayside entirely.

I sympathize. When I was in business school at UCLA's Anderson School, and some professors talked about "fuzzy" topics such as organizational behavior, I didn't take it particularly seriously. I was more interested in great products and driving revenue (little did I know that a great culture really helps these things). Yet, as I got back out into the work world and experienced different cultures firsthand, and once I started running my own businesses and coaching others, I began to see the difference an intentionally designed culture has on growth and the bottom line. Plus, it wasn't just the financials being impacted—culture has an incredible effect on how it feels to own and run a business. It is also one of the biggest factors in attracting and retaining top talent.

This chapter will do three things to help you see these differences for yourself and begin to see how you can sculpt your own culture for the better. First, we'll look at the differences between "default mode" cultures and intentionally designed cultures. Then, I'll walk you through defining and designing your own high-performance culture. Finally, we'll talk about *employer* branding, which is particularly important to small and midsize businesses that may not realize the extent to which top talent is pre-screening *them* before applying for or accepting a position. Along the way, we'll address key culture myths and some steps you can take to repair a culture that isn't what you want it to be.

Why "Culture by Design" Matters

Culture by design, as a term, is something I got from the legendary executive, sales coach, and adventurer Jack Daly. Another legend, entrepreneur Norm Brodsky, says every business has a culture, whether you plan it or not. It's a total myth to think that your business doesn't have a personality or vibe that's unique to the organization. The difference is that some businesses have a culture that "just happened," and some businesses have a culture that's been intentionally built and cultivated.

So, when you start looking at any company culture, there are two key questions to ask:

1. Is this company's culture an accident or intentional?
2. Is this culture a healthy, good culture?

It's also not enough to simply have good intentions around culture. My businesses are a perfect case in point for this. When I founded the NYER in 2003, I was coming off a bad experience at my last job and thinking a lot about what kind of culture I wanted at NYER. I even put a lot of my thoughts down on paper because I wanted to have a great culture. However, once things got moving with the business, my priority switched to driving revenue. Ultimately, we did have a *decent* culture, but it wasn't anything like what I had envisioned, and it wasn't anything I'd actively built or shaped.

In contrast, when Andrew and I started WBN, we started with our core values, and the very first one was a commitment to putting talent first. That, and our other core values, have shaped our culture and success to date.

WBN's Core Values

- Put our talent first
- Work with integrity and transparency
- Work with an ownership mentality
- Have a growth mindset
- Work with an excellent attitude
- Pursue excellence

Every part of our business—how we hire, manage, retain, release, and reward—links back to these core values *intentionally*. There's no mystery about our priorities, no confusion about what's right or wrong in our environment, and no doubt about how we're supposed to show up as an organization to our staff and our customers.

And it's working. Our culture drives performance, and the results speak for themselves. We've earned a spot on the 2024 *Inc. Power Partner* list—a recognition based on feedback directly from our customers—and we're proud of our industry-leading Net Promoter Score (NPS) and Employee Net Promoter Score (eNPS). These aren't just metrics to us; they're proof that building a culture by design leads to happier teams, more loyal clients, and sustainable growth.

As a result, once things were rolling, the leadership team didn't need to do a lot of heavy lifting on the culture side. We have an incredible culture, and it's driven by the team. They organically talk about our values in team meetings and as they collaborate. They're bought into the culture those values represent, and they bring it to life each day, which expresses itself in extremely high performance, extremely happy customers, and a rate of growth that's catapulted us up the *Inc. 5000* listings.

Defining Your Culture

Within your organization, there's a lot you can do to define and improve on your current culture. After all, one of the best things about culture is that it's a living phenomenon that you can shape over time. So, if it's not already in great shape, you can absolutely take steps to get it there.

Identify Your Own Core Company Values

One of the first steps you should take is to identify your core company values. What are the anchors in your business ethos? Which beliefs guide your daily actions—or what would you *like* to guide your daily actions? Get your thoughts down, and then reach out for input from the rest of your team. Pay special attention to thoughts on culture from your current top performers and A-players.

It's okay if your core values are a bit aspirational and something you want to reach for from where you are presently, as long as you and your team are committing to getting there.

Company culture isn't a team luncheon or a ping pong table—it's the water your team swims in, the way people feel about working at your company. Do they wake up in the morning energized to start the day? Do they believe they're contributing to something greater than themselves? Do they enjoy spending time with their coworkers? Do they see a future here?

A strong culture acts as a powerful magnet, attracting top talent and customers alike. It signals to prospective employees that your company is a place where they can find belonging and purpose—naturally attracting candidates who are aligned with your values and inspired by your mission. That, in turn, permeates every client touchpoint... turning culture into a competitive edge and separating the ping pong tables from the truly remarkable.

—Shawn Busse, Founder of Kinesis, a growth studio for
owner-operated businesses

Live Your Core Values in a Practical, Tangible Way

Once you've identified your core company values, it's time to LIVE those values. This is not a woo-woo concept I'm throwing out here. Living your values as a company translates into some very practical and tangible behaviors for managers and employees alike.

For example, when you see team members work towards your values or exhibit the attitudes you value, it's a time for praise and celebration. This can be built into regular performance review touchpoints or honored with in-the-moment elements of recognition. It works as a great reinforcement with employees of all generations, but it's especially impactful for Millennial and Gen Z staff because those cohorts have a preference for frequent feedback, guidance, and recognition in their work. When your company lives the values and celebrates the values, you make this aspect of management easier while also giving staff what they crave from the work relationship, too.

At WBN, we've established what we call the "W Awards." This has been a very popular program. It's also very easy to administer and very low cost. Basically, anyone in the company can nominate anybody else in the company for going above and beyond their role or their responsibilities in a way that ties back to one of our core values. Management reviews these nominations on a weekly basis. There's a small monetary award, but more importantly, recipients are recognized on the weekly all-staff call. You should see the looks on people's faces when they get recognized! It's priceless.

To read more about our W Awards and how the program works with our fully remote team, check out our full write-up at https://www.workbetternow.com/ blog/how-workbetternow-recognizes-its-remote-team or by scanning the QR code below:

Programs like this are particularly important when you're running a hybrid team or a fully-remote operation. People want to feel like they're a part of something that matters and a part of an organization that cares enough about them to notice what they're doing and recognize a good job. They get excited, and then they become drivers of the whole system. It's not something we're pushing hard from the top down. It's a positivity, enthusiasm, and engagement that's spread throughout the organization and led by the employees themselves.

On top of all this, programs like this reinforce our core values by celebrating the people who put them into practice and embody them every day.

Provide Correction and Coaching to the Values

Identifying your core company values and striving to live those values also provides you with a solid framework for corrections and identifying when you have team members who aren't a great fit for your team. You want your talent to live your values. That's a clear statement and not an ambiguous performance metric to establish.

So, when anyone in your company sees behavior or attitudes that run counter to your values, you can address that in a 3-step process. Step one, you let the person know they've done something that is not consistent with your company's values. Give specific examples of where things weren't right and how they can improve. Where appropriate and where you have the staff availability, pair them up with a strong performer for peer coaching and mentorship. Often, one conversation will be enough because high performers can self-correct and rapidly adapt.

Now, if it does continue to happen, the next step is a more formal warning. Then, if you still have a situation where this particular team member isn't willing or able to live your organization's values, you can have the conversation about allowing them to find a better home for their skills somewhere else. It's not vague, it's not subjective, and it's not personal. It's "these are the ways you continue to not live our values, and so because of these behaviors, it's time to go."

This moment of separation is often a point of worry for small and midsize business owners. You have a small team, and staff changes can have big impacts. However, this values-focused approach is different. You are what you tolerate, and your staff members are watching how you handle things when there's someone who isn't a good fit or who has a bad attitude toward the work. The reality is that your A-players don't want to work with C-players, either. So, you'll find there's a lot of internal support for helping bad fits move on quickly.

Improving A Less Than Ideal Culture

Coaching to your values, living them, and celebrating culture wins can be difficult when your culture isn't where you want it to be. Fortunately, you can take steps to acknowledge where you're at now culturally and transition toward a better state.

Like many things in business, leadership matters here. A company's culture is always a direct reflection of its leadership. Leaders should take a hard look in the mirror and conduct a thorough self-assessment. Understanding yourself and how you behave in the workplace is crucial because your actions set the tone for the entire organization.

From there, you can lean on well-established tools like the benchmark engagement survey provided by SurveyMonkey. Add a few customized questions for your organization, as needed. Then, study the results to learn what about the culture keeps people with you, which values are aligned, and which values are not being adhered to or may need improvement. This will give you a sound baseline for what's important to your staff currently, and what changes you need to make to build on your strengths as you intentionally pivot toward activities, behaviors, and operational systems that nourish and improve your culture alignment.

Developing Your Employer Brand

Along with your culture, you will want to spend time working on your employer brand.

To understand your employer brand, step back and reflect on your company brand. Basically, this is what people say about your company when you're not in the room. Current and former customers have a set of beliefs about you, as do your peers and competitors in the industry.

So, your employer brand is what current, former, and prospective *employees* think and say about your company as a place to work. This is chatter when you're not in the room, and it's more important than ever. Why? Simple– instead of spreading person-to-person via word of mouth as it once would have, these days it's on display for everybody to see on sites like Glassdoor, where current and former employees can leave public reviews of you.

These reviews matter because prospective employees look at these reviews. Highly sought-after talent are going to have options when it comes to employers.

Now, these employer reviews can catch you by surprise. At WBN, we've been caught by surprise. We were so focused on our culture and growth that we did not pay attention to this for the first few years. Then, when we did look at our Glassdoor rating, we found that it was not reflective of what we saw as our employer brand. Remember that, typically, those who review, especially when it comes to job-related reviews, are the ones who have not had a great experience.

So, we took action. We asked our current employees to post their thoughts on Glassdoor. We didn't tell them what to say or coach them on the reviews they should leave. We simply prompted them to share the truth about their experiences, and our rating and review balance went to something that we thought was more appropriately reflective of our employer brand.

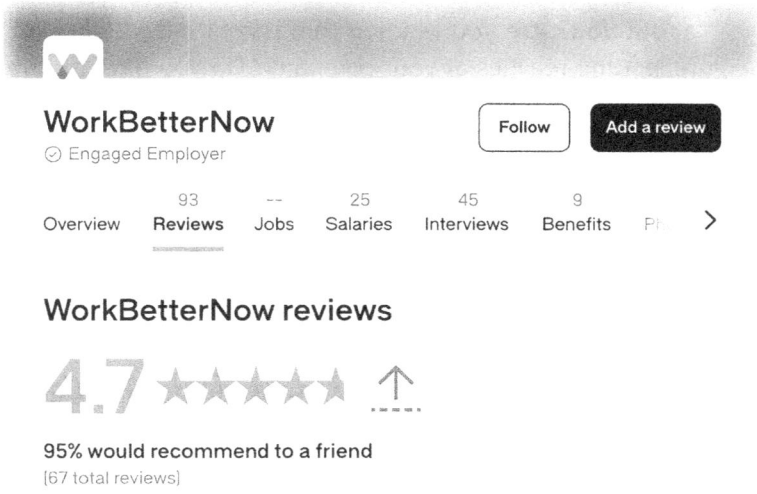

If that kind of surprise can happen to a company like ours, where we intentionally put talent first and actively try to live our values, imagine what's happening elsewhere. Many, many business owners don't think to ever look at these kinds of reviews. They should because these reviews matter, and candidates are reading them. If your reviews aren't an accurate reflection of your brand, then you need to take action to improve your reputation by encouraging employees to share more, making structural changes to your employee experiences, or investing in marketing to ensure your story is being told properly.

Action Step: Check Your Reviews

If you don't know your company's current employer brand, now is the time to find out. Take a moment to look up your firm on Glassdoor. What is being said about you? Are you reading things that accurately reflect the realities at your company? Do you have a reputation you could lean on for recruiting top talent, or is there room for improvement?

Your Culture, Your Brand, and Your Future

A good culture isn't something you can allow to spring up organically and hope it springs up in the right way. You need to actively shape it so you have the kind of organization you want and the kind of organization you actually enjoy running.

Moving away from being a "default mode" organization also has a big impact on your employer brand. Top talent can—and will—check your reputation before they come to work for you. You need to make sure your online reviews and public employer brand accurately reflect your story and where your business is headed.

The good news? When you invest time in these things, everything else gets easier. Culture solves a ton of problems around interpersonal dynamics, job performance, and performance management. It can help you get the right people interested in walking through your door, and it can help you keep the right people with your organization for the long term. To borrow from a well-known proverb: "The best time to plant a tree was 20 years ago. The second best time is now." In other words, the best time to create your culture was on Day One. The second-best time? Today.

That long-term side of things—keeping the people you're attracting and hiring—is vital to your success. Retention is where your hard work on culture pays off for you, though culture is not the only ingredient in a strong retention rate. As you process everything you've learned so far about culture and brand, let's push forward and look at what it takes to ensure your future success with a powerful retention program.

CHAPTER 4

Retaining Today's Top Talent

"Clients do not come first. Employees come first. If you take care of your employees, they will take care of the clients."
– Richard Branson

In today's competitive talent market, keeping your top performers—the A-players—is crucial for success. Yet your top employees are likely on somebody's list of people they want to hire, and, accordingly, they'll be constantly courted by other firms. To play to win in this environment, your retention strategies need to be a strong and constant force. You need to build the kind of workplace where someone could approach one of your top performers with an offer... and they would get turned down.

In this chapter, we'll look at what it takes to make that a believable reality. Some tactics may be things you've heard about before, but I will show you how to apply them in new ways that align with how modern talent responds to incentives, development opportunities, and paths to advancement. By the end of the chapter, you should have a great understanding of how to put these strategies to work for your company.

Of course, everything we've already discussed applies. You need to have a healthy internal culture. You need to be the type of organization that quickly removes bad apples (as I've mentioned, A-players don't like being around C-players). Above all, you need to be the kind of organization where top performers can see themselves growing and thriving for years to come.

Now, you might be thinking that all of this is a lot to do, and the ultimate success seems far off. I can appreciate this. That said, the sooner you start, the sooner you will start to reap the benefits. Think of progress, not perfection. Plus, momentum is an undeniable force in this—once you get things moving in the right direction, it can become a self-reinforcing power for improvement.

Paying for Great Talent– Why Compensation Is Your Insurance Policy

There are some problems in business that you can solve with money. Too many SMBs think that in retention, money is the ultimate solution. That's not true, although competitive compensation—and, at times, overcompensation—does have a role to play.

What do I mean by overcompensation? I'm not implying that you should be paying people more than they'll ever be worth to you. I simply want you to have protection against losing star talent.

Top performers should earn top-level salaries and bonuses commensurate with their skills. The idea of additional premium pay—what some might call "overcompensation"—is actually an insurance policy for you. It's a way of considering the cost of replacement when looking at your talent.

Calculating the True Costs of A-Level Attrition

With a talent poacher, you know one of the first moves is offering your talent more than they currently make. If they accept that outside offer, you now have to deal with all the costs and hassle of finding their replacement. This can be devastating, especially considering the tightness of the labor market.

After all, recovering from the departure of a top performer isn't just about replacing that one person. You also have to account for all the bandwidth it sucks up to advertise the role, do multiple rounds of interviews, get a new hire in place, onboard them, get them familiar with your organization and your clients, and coach them up on their performance. All the while, there's the risk that this new person will be a poor fit, and you'll have to start over again from scratch.

Plus, in addition to your costs in replacing them, you need to consider the lost value of their work while their role stands vacant. HR studies put the value of an employee at one to three times their annual salary.[9] So, an average employee you're paying $75,000 might offer you $150,000 in value.

Take that 150,000 and divide it by 260—the average number of working days per year. This gives you an HR metric known as Cost of Vacancy or COV. Your $75,000 employee who brings you $150,000 in value carries a COV of $576.92 per day, or around $17,300 in COV costs per month.

Most small and midsize businesses aren't considering COV. However, it's a number I've found very motivating in prioritizing retention and helping you rethink your overall compensation tactics. In the context of COV, it's easy to see how offering top performers a wage or special bonus that puts their compensation right at the top or even above market rates may actually save you serious money over the long term by helping keep your turnover rates low.

In fact, as I reflect on some of the biggest successful small and midsize business exits shared with me by people I know and friends of mine, several of them "overpaid" their top talent, or to an outsider, they seem overpaid. Why? It mitigates the business risks we've just discussed and helps you, as a business owner, sleep better at night.

Of course, you can't rely on money alone to keep someone with you. Cash doesn't fully offset a toxic culture, overwork, or unfulfilling work. Top-quality talent doesn't want to stick in a dead-end role, even if the salary is sky-high. Many high performers willingly accept roles that pay less to get a culture fit they prefer, more flexibility, more personal fulfillment, or more potential for development and growth. This is why, although cash compensation does matter, it's not the only thing you need to consider when addressing retention.

Let Your Talent See Their Potential to Grow with You

A huge element of retention is letting talent see their potential with your organization. Some 86% of employees would consider switching jobs for better growth opportunities, while some 94% would stick around longer if their company offered them chances to advance, according to CloudTask.[10]

This ties back into the younger generation's preferences for fast advancement, but it's relevant to any ambitious employee in your organization. Good people will leave if they don't feel there's a rewarding future for them at your firm. So, you want to think about the advancement opportunities you have available and how you can communicate the availability of those opportunities to your team.

I feel very strongly that career advancement discussions should happen at least once a year with every member of your team. You can talk about where they'd like to be, and the skills they would need to get there, or the behaviors they'd need to exhibit. There will be times, of course, when expectations and ambitions are going to be a stretch. There may also be times when the next step up simply isn't available within your organization. However, you don't want career advancement to be an afterthought in your talent development or retention. It is usually easier to train up a good worker you already like than to find their replacement on the open market.

Show Off Your Flexibility

Another point of communication you don't want to be an afterthought when it comes to retention is your organization's flexibility and commitment to work/life balance. This has become a hot issue with workers of all ages, and it's particularly key to keeping workers who may be members of the "sandwich generation" with both young children at home and caregiving responsibilities for elderly parents.

A hundred years ago, it was normal to work 60+ hours a week, and as little as a decade ago, the concept of remote work was still relatively rare. Fast forward a few years through several technological leaps and one worldwide pandemic, and commuting to an office where you spend 8+ hours each day is no longer a universal norm. Millions of people have had the taste of working from home, of having the freedom to duck out for a quick errand or appointment, and of spending more time with their families because they don't have to commute.

So, if you have an organization where hybrid work systems or fully remote structures will work, offer that to both prospective and current employees. It helps attract great talent—which we'll discuss more in the next chapter—and it helps keep your existing talent. After all, who wants to leave a great job that fits nicely into the rhythm of their daily life? In a 2024 survey of U.S. workers, just over half indicated they would be willing to take a pay cut of up to 20% to get a better quality of life.[11]

Demonstrate Good Management Frameworks

Conversations about career advancement opportunities and flexibility in scheduling also allow you to demonstrate to your talent that you have good management frameworks in place. These can be vital for retention, as they provide assurances to top performers that they won't be trapped under a micromanager, and that they will be rewarded for their results instead of just the hours they spend chained to their laptops.

For example, 15 years ago, I was in an office with a full team, watching how everybody was working. Now, at WBN, my company is 100% remote. We can't watch people work, and frankly, we don't want to be doing that anyway.

As an organization, we truly have no desire to know how everybody's working, minute to minute or hour to hour. All we care about is living our core values and the results our team can achieve. That's it.

Operationally, this is supported by the management frameworks we have put in place. For us, following the Entrepreneurial Operating System (EOS) framework has been a game-changer. Everyone has a set of key performance indicators (KPIs), and each week, we review those KPIs in addition to their progress on their quarterly big "rocks" projects. It keeps us focused on the right things without getting derailed or pulled down into the minutiae of day-to-day activities.

Now, there are many proven frameworks other than the EOS available to you. The point here is to have a system in place to track results so everyone is on the same page and managers do not need to micromanage. This also helps to create a positive culture. As LeiLani Quiray, Founder and CEO of be the change HR, Inc., notes, you can't just go straight to your employees and say, "I need you to be busier." Instead, she recommends building a culture of trust and respect and clearly defining expectations.

Building a culture around trust and respect creates an environment where employees feel valued and trusted to get the work done. This trust needs to be mutual between leadership and employees. When employees feel trusted, they are more likely to be engaged and productive, and you won't have to worry about issues like "time theft."

This starts before the hire. A well-defined job description that outlines exactly what's expected is vital – and you want to have that in place *before* you hire for the role. From there, you can develop the appropriate performance metrics that will help you measure productivity and success. These metrics provide a clear and reasonable standard for what good performance looks like and help you create a work environment where your employees are both engaged and performing at their best.

Invest in Upskilling Them for the Ultimate Win-Win-Win

A final retention tactic I want to touch on here is upskilling. Upskilling, with respect to existing employees, means training them on new skills. That training can be internal, conducted by a member of the team, or you can pay for them to get certain certifications or to take specific classes.

Upskilling is a win-win-win proposition. First, you know the pace of business change is accelerating. This means, among other things, that you need to bring new capabilities to your company to keep up. We'll go over a framework for that in Chapter 8, with AI and automation as our examples. Naturally, to lean into a framework like that, you've got to have staff who can rise to that challenge, and investing in upskilling provides you with that.

At the same time, you have employees with ambitions. They want to earn more, they want to get promoted, they want to feel like they're developing and growing. Upskilling speaks directly to that and allows employees to become worth the extra seniority and pay they desire. Finally, by investing in your talent, you're demonstrating pretty visibly that you value them and want to keep them around, which has a huge impact on both performance and retention. Win, win, win.

How does this work in practice? I'll share three examples here. They'll give you an idea of what's possible with smart upskilling investments and drive home that you should really never care where somebody starts with you, since talented people will go places.

- At WBN, our very first employee outside of the ownership team was my assistant, Jessica. We have continuously invested in growing her skillset, and it's paid off for both of us. She now serves as the General Manager of the company.

- Our Director of IT and Special Projects at WBN, Silvana, also started as my partner Andrew's assistant. She's very focused on technology, and we are big believers in leveraging tech so that we can scale, improve the customer experience, and reduce cycle times. Helping her strengthen her skill set has helped her grow in the organization, and it's benefited us by expanding our capabilities as well.

- At Dropoff, a WBN client, we placed Estefania as an Administrative Assistant. Within 18 months, she had learned (internally) to manage tickets and address client needs on a broader scale. This allowed her to move up within their organization and become their Regional Operations Assistant.

Closing Thoughts on Retention...

You can never assume that your current talent will stay with you. Top performers have options, so you want to make your organization their personal employer of choice.

Winning the retention game isn't strictly about money. Yes, you should pay a competitive wage and even be willing to go above the market to keep your best team members from leaving. However, you can't rely on dollars to do all the heavy lifting. Today's talent also wants to see opportunities for advancement, space for work/life balance, good management frameworks, and opportunities to upskill themselves with you.

It doesn't happen automatically. It takes intention and effort. Done right, though, you can see your retention rates drop, and your best performers truly thrive. This, in turn, builds up your reputation and brand as a first-rate employer, helping you attract more of the people you want to have join your organization.

CHAPTER 5

The New Way to Attract Great Talent

"Acquiring the right talent is the most important key to growth...
Hiring was—and still is—the most important thing we do."
– Mark Benioff

Small and midsize businesses are not great at recruitment and hiring. I'll just say it—they are typically terrible at it. I know I was. While I have made many terrific hires over the years, my batting average is certainly not hall-of-fame worthy. It was a weakness, but that doesn't mean it needs to be an ongoing weakness of yours.

Even if you consider recruitment and hiring to be strengths, there's no denying that a lot has changed since the pandemic. How people want to be recruited has shifted, how people respond has changed, and how people expect to be hired and onboarded has changed. You can't rest on your laurels—it's a landscape that demands constant evolution to keep up.

The good news? You *can* attract great talent to your business and win them over to your team. So far, we've talked about the importance of designing a culture where talent wants to be and what you'll need to do to ensure you can retain the talent you attract. Now, I will share some other key steps you can take to land top talent.

Optimizing Your Recruitment Process

On the sales side of any successful company, I have an obsession with making it simple for people to buy from you. Prospects should be able to express interest and then swiftly move through your funnels to becoming a customer without getting hung up in forms, extra steps, or painful bits of unnecessary stuff.

That's pretty obvious, right? Yet when I propose to small and midsize business owners that they take the same obsession over to their application and hiring processes, it is a head scratcher for many. Many still think there is a "buyer's market" with candidates who can't wait to work for their company.

To be quite blunt, the best talent out there is shopping around for the best opportunity, and they can afford to be picky.

If your position descriptions are short on detail and your open postings are little more than word salad templates, good candidates will skip right over you. Your postings need to be persuasive descriptions that accurately describe the role, expectations, and the specific skills and experience required. Accuracy is key—the more specific you are about what the job actually entails, the more likely you are to attract the right candidates. And don't stop there. Highlight your culture, values, and opportunities for growth.

If top candidates choose to apply with you, but the process is a total pain, with repetitive steps and having to fill out the same information in multiple forms, it's the same as a prospective buyer who encounters hurdles and friction when they try to complete their purchase with you. They're more likely to pull an "abandon cart" than to follow through.

The same will happen to you if your process is slow. Top talent generally gets a new role after just 10 days of actively seeking employment, according to 2024 data from Zippia.[12] That's your window—10 days. Much like customers looking for fast shipping, candidates are looking for fast offers. So, if your hiring process takes multiple weeks or months, look at what you can do to speed things up. You don't want to skip valuable vetting steps, but things like scheduling interviews quickly, group interviews for early rounds, or interviewing multiple top candidates the same day may help you shorten your window and be able to move faster on hiring the best talent.

Recruiting Perspectives: Candidate-Friendly Best Practices

According to LeiLani Quiray, Founder and CEO of be the change HR, Inc., a candidate-friendly recruitment process starts with a deep understanding of the job itself. Often, when organizations have an open position, they rush to fill it, sometimes without fully grasping what the role entails. Before anything else, it's crucial to know exactly what you're hiring for, what the person will be doing, and what's truly required for success in the role. Be realistic in these expectations to set a solid foundation for recruitment.

Another key practice from Quiray is to set realistic job requirements. She's seen many roles where the listed qualifications don't align with what's actually necessary. For instance, does an administrative role really require a bachelor's degree? By reassessing what's truly needed, you open the door to a wider range of candidates. This approach can also promote diversity, giving more people the opportunity to grow in their careers.

Lastly, Quiray recommends that in interviews, you focus on questions that will assess how the candidate aligns with your company's culture.

Laura Crothers, CEO of Crothers HR Consulting, likes employee referral programs, where you're incentivizing employees to "recruit" for you. Employees know the culture and vet the candidates to ensure they have strong coworkers.

She also recommends that if several people are interviewing the candidate, you should start the process with everyone involved together and ask the basic background questions that all the interviewers want to know. Then, after that initial 20 minutes, the candidate spends time with each person 1-on-1 to go deeper into the area that they are responsible for learning about. This saves the candidate time and prevents them from feeling like a broken record. It also allows the candidate to take one half-day or full day off work and not have to take time on different days for different interviews.

Finally, she says that it's important for candidates who were at least phone screened to be communicated with frequently to understand the process and where they stand. If the hiring manager has eliminated that candidate, they should be told so they are not waiting around, hopeful for weeks.

Good candidates are looking for signs you've got what they want and can live up to your promises. Remember, A-players don't want to work with C-players, and if the A-player you want thinks you're a C-player kind of company, you don't stand a chance. If your process is shoddy, candidates might assume that this is an indication of what it is like to work at your company.

So, audit your recruitment, application, and hiring processes. Yes, there will be things you can't change for compliance or legal reasons, but you may be surprised at how much you can do to streamline your processes and reduce the friction in your recruitment efforts.

Now, I'm not suggesting that you want to rush things along just for the sake of speed. You want to take an appropriate amount of time to make a good decision, do assessments, and hold interviews with key stakeholders and future managers.

However, imagine your customers going through the same process. How would you improve it for them?

Here's what Larry Zogby, CEO of RDS Same Day Delivery, does to lead better interviews and ensure smooth onboarding:

"In my four decades of experience, I've learned that a resume doesn't tell the whole story [in interviews]. I focus on building trust quickly and engaging in a genuine conversation to understand a candidate's story, goals, and passions. I listen with both my heart and my head, looking for cultural fit, curiosity, attitude, and ambition. This approach helps me identify the qualities that will thrive in a remote environment.

My executive assistant also joins all interviews for remote hires to provide a point of contact for the successful candidates during onboarding. New hires receive two weeks of customer service training with her, join a group chat, and attend 15-minute meet-and-greets with offshore and in-office teams. After training, they transition to their department for role-specific training. I check in weekly with both the new hire and the team to ensure a smooth process."

Make Room for Upskilling as a Part of Your Recruitment Model

A final way to get more great talent coming to you is to leverage upskilling as you recruit. In the last chapter, I discussed the win-win-win role upskilling can play in your retention strategy.

Upskilling can also help you hire faster, widen your talent pool, and ensure a better likelihood of finding a great cultural fit.

It is indeed very rare to find a prospect that ticks every requirement. Most people—even very good people advanced in their careers—have skill gaps. At WBN, we see this quite often with requirements for experience in specific software. Companies will often say, "Must have Salesforce or HubSpot experience." And most of the time, insisting on these requirements is a mistake, as these skills can be quickly learned via internal or external training. During the interview, ask about how they've learned new systems, and you'll be in a good position to gauge whether they can learn the systems you use in a short period of time.

If you make upskilling a part of your recruitment and hiring plans, intending to invest and grow people's skills, it broadens the talent available to you and makes it easier for you to get a good base of talent through the door. You never want to compromise on the culture fit aspect, but being more flexible around hard skills that can be trained up expands your hiring pool. At WBN, we have had tremendous success with this approach, as have our clients.

Don't forget to include your onboarding system in your audit as well. Research shows that talent forms their deepest and strongest opinions about your organization within the first 40 hours of employment.[13] Make it fun. Make it meaningful. Make it something that makes them happy with their choice, excited to be a part of your team, and a more loyal and engaged new hire right from their very first week.

As we touched on with retention, it's not important what role serves as the starting point. Where someone comes in is irrelevant to where they can go, especially if they are ambitious, adaptable, and eager to acquire new skills and knowledge. Their path up through your organization will energize and motivate them and help you build up a reputation as a great place to work and attract people who are serious about growth and success.

The overall result? You'll be able to become an employer-of-choice for a broader, deeper pool of talent... including a pool of talent you may not have realized could be available to you, which I'll showcase for you in the chapter ahead.

CHAPTER 6

Expanding Your Talent Pool: The Remote Advantage

"One of the secret benefits of using remote workers is that the work itself becomes the yardstick to judge someone's performance."
— Jason Fried, Co-founder, Basecamp

Building your Dream Team requires access to a broader, deeper pool of candidates—far beyond what you can access in your immediate geography. Above all, you need to get access to talent that's interested, motivated, and enthusiastic about doing great work for you.

Naturally, I'm talking about the potential of remote talent, something I'm a big proponent of using. However, I'm not such a cheerleader for remote talent that I believe it's right for all businesses and situations. There's a certain amount of discernment and a number of organizational fit considerations that go into making remote talent a viable solution.

Right now, I'd like to walk through those nuances with you. We will cover how remote talent makes sense broadly in today's tight labor markets, how to judge if it makes sense for your company, and the best practices for incorporating remote workers into your operations.

Why Remote Work Makes Sense in Today's Labor Markets

At this point, you've learned enough about today's (and tomorrow's) talent situation to understand that small and midsize businesses are facing a talent crisis. You need people— hard-working, talented people—that are incredibly difficult to find. They become even harder to find when you restrict your search radius to those people living within a "reasonable commute" of your physical office.

There are, obviously, some jobs that just have to be done on-site. However, with the rise of cloud-based computing, widespread availability of high-speed internet, and multiple online collaboration tools like office suites, chats, task managers, and video conferencing spaces, an ever-increasing number of roles have become geographically independent.

Aside from my office in New York, we have no physical offices and are a fully remote organization. Our people (45 at the time I write this) are at home—homes that crisscross North and South America. This allows everyone to be in their most comfortable and productive space while also allowing the company as a whole to source the best talent from the broadest possible area that makes sense for us.

What do our clients think about all this? They're on board. So much so that they have hired over 500 WBN Certified Professionals™ who work from their homes throughout Latin America (at the time I write this). And most of our clients will tell you that, since adding the right remote employees, their overall productivity has gone up considerably.

It Works for Others, but Could Remote Work for You?

It's one thing to hear about the opportunity of remote work and a remote talent pool, and quite another thing to imagine implementing it yourself. Many small and midsize businesses hesitate when they should push forward, worried about how it would work. Let's look at some of the biggest potential issues together right now.

One major objection to remote work that I hear concerns a general lack of oversight of the talent. You can't see them. You have no idea if they're working or not, right? How can you be confident they're doing the work they say they're doing?

To this I always reply, just look at the results. You shouldn't be micromanaging your employees or monitoring their every move when they're remote—or when they're in the office. It's not the best use of your precious time. Instead, if you implement smart management frameworks, as we mentioned in Chapter 4 and Chapter 5, the same kinds of weekly staff meetings and touchbase sessions you would have in a physical office can be equally effective for managing and supporting employee performance.

Another worry that I hear is that a remote team wouldn't work in your culture. Fair enough—if your in-office culture is broken, you can't expect miracles in a remote culture, either. So, just as we touched on with recruitment and retention, you need to do the culture work first before you can reasonably expect a remote framework to succeed. Then again, you need to fix your culture for your company to succeed, whether you have remote talent or not.

One aspect of the culture to keep in mind, though, is whether the talent you're considering will thrive in a remote environment. Humans are social creatures on a sliding scale, with some of us very much needing the physical presence of others throughout the day to be happy and do our best work. You can screen for this in interviews by asking people to highlight their favorite elements of their past jobs or how they have worked independently for extended periods. Your main goal is simply to ensure that you're not putting someone into a remote position when they thrive off of being shoulder to shoulder with co-workers or need the collaborative energy of a busy office.

I also hear companies express concern about making the technology work with a remote team. However, most small and midsize businesses use cloud-based systems today, and most work takes place within shared software environments where geography is no real barrier to access. Your IT department or IT support team should also be able to handle any security or secure access concerns—this is definitely a space where the tech frameworks needed to have a remote and global workforce are well-established, so as a small or midsize business considering it, you don't need to reinvent the wheel on the technology side of things.

Finally, some small and midsize businesses do have concerns about the tax and jurisdictional implications of expanding out of their immediate geography by adding remote talent to the team. Fortunately, this is fairly easy today as most HR and payroll systems will do much of the heavy lifting for you. That said, you should speak with your tax advisor and HR attorney to ensure you are compliant with state and local regulations.

Maximizing the Performance of Your Remote Talent

How you manage your remote talent dramatically impacts their performance of the work, and there's a certain art to it. Fortunately, many things that help remote team members excel also help in-office staff do their best work. So, learning about these skills and best practices will benefit you even if you ultimately decide against building a remote team.

Open and Frequent Communication is Critical

Clear, open, and frequent communication is critical to making a remote environment work. It's important with in-office teams, but you will need to do more with remote talent because your remote talent isn't picking up anything other than what you say to them. There's no water cooler where they can absorb office norms and breaking news from their colleagues, so you want to make sure you're particularly clear and perhaps even "over communicating" to ensure your expectations, needs, and task details are being heard and understood.

When I took classes by Peter Guber, the legendary entrepreneur, he noted that a lot of people go through life confused. He used the term "mutual mystification," which means that neither party in a conversation is clear about what is expected or going on. They're not sure what's happening or what their role is. Many problems with remote talent tie directly back to this—where there's confusion, you will get frustration and subpar performance or results that aren't in line with your expectations. So, communicate upfront and often about your expectations and norms around things such as:

- Working hours: When do you expect talent to be online and responsive? What should happen if they need to step away for a short break or a longer appointment? What constitutes "out of office" for the remote team, and how should that be communicated?

- Key contacts: Who does what on your team? Who do they report to? Who decides on new projects, assigns them, and monitors their completion? Who should remote talent reach out to if they have a problem with a task or with a client? What's their authority for in-the-moment calls, and when and how should they escalate things?

- Work tools: What platforms and systems make your company work? When do you use email, when do you use chat, and what task management systems are in play? Does everyone have full access and understand how to use the tools in front of them? Where can they find other resources if they need them?

- Success in role: What does success look like for your remote talent? Whether you're using the EOS framework or another system with KPIs, everyone should be able to describe what success on a project looks like and what success in the role looks like from both a quantitative and qualitative perspective. What's average performance, and what's going above and beyond?

When you have made this all very clear, you will get better work and create a less stressful environment for getting work done.

Performance Management

In addition to setting up good communication lines, you'll also want to have solid performance management frameworks in place. They don't have to be overly complex or burdensome— just enough KPIs to help you and your talent stay aligned about what's being done and how the work is being completed.

For example, at WBN, as I've mentioned, we use the EOS framework. So, we have weekly L10 meetings for each department, a weekly all-staff meeting, weekly or bi-weekly one-on-ones with direct reports, and interdepartmental meetings as it makes sense. Among other things, at L10s, we go through everyone's KPIs and projects so we know early on, when things are "off-track." You may adopt the same framework or a different one, but whatever you choose, it should be used consistently.

This kind of regular, consistent contact is particularly meaningful for remote talent, as they're not with you in person to absorb news or instructions outside of what is communicated to them directly. The more you can do to keep them feeling connected and in alignment with the overall mission and goals, the easier it will be for them to see how their work and their task performance impact the broader company mission. You'll also have more chances to provide continuous feedback to them, something I prefer to the practice of saving everything for a quarterly or even annual review.

Finally, as I've touched on before, you should have at least one annual conversation with your team members about their larger ambitions and goals. This will help you see how they may be able to grow within your organization, what training or upskilling might be appropriate for them, and how you may be able to harness their personal ambitions and desires for professional development in the service of your company's own objectives for scaling, growth, and expansion.

Enable Connections Between Staff Members and Build an Inclusive Culture

A last key element of maximizing remote talent performance centers around your culture and your interconnections between team members.

A mistake I see some small and midsize businesses make with remote talent is keeping that talent off in a silo from the rest of the staff. This can cause communication breakdowns, gaps in customer service experiences, and a sense of isolation that can cost you the remote talent as well as build alienation with your in-office staff. So, a better move is to consciously and intentionally work to build up an interconnected culture.

In practical terms, here are a few things you can do to make this happen:

- On team calls, put up a video screen so remote staff can "sit at the table" with your in-office staff
- Ensure any brainstorming boards, vision boards, or to-do lists are available in the cloud (as opposed to, say, being up on the whiteboard in your physical conference room, where remote staff can't clearly see or reference them—unless that is on camera as well)
- Give space for remote team members to share their successes and wins, just as in-office staff would do
- Host virtual happy hours, lunch-and-learns, or online team-building sessions that both remote and in-office staff can attend

You can also look for opportunities to periodically get together in the same physical space. Some small and midsize businesses host annual or even quarterly all-hands meetings where they fly everyone to an offsite location for a company retreat or goal-planning sessions. This can be particularly impactful for firms that have gone fully remote, where no one is generally in the same physical space and may never have met face-to-face.

At WBN, where we have people in over a dozen countries, we've built fun and team-building activities into our regular weekly team meetings, weekly department meetings, and weekly or biweekly check-ins. So, we have fun stuff like virtual happy hours, virtual meditation sessions, and virtual talent shows. This has led to a great culture where friendships are born remotely and translate to real life. Many members of our team travel inside and across borders to hang out with each other. In addition, our leadership team meets in Latin America (as half of them are located there) twice a year.

The more you can do to build a united culture, an inclusive culture, and a culture that says "we all work together," the better your results and performance from your remote talent will be. They'll feel valued, you'll know how to get the best from them, and your bottom-line results will show the impact of your efforts.

How Remote Talent Can Transform Your Business

By employing remote talent, you gain access to a broader, deeper pool of candidates. You can get talent that might otherwise be out of reach, both geographically and financially. With the right tech tools and management frameworks (e.g., EOS), you can unlock high performance while lessening the supervisory burden. This helps you get what you need from your remote talent on an ongoing and mutually satisfactory basis.

All in all, remote talent makes good sense for small and midsize businesses that may be struggling to find good people locally or who are being priced out of their usual geographic markets. Formerly reserved only for large multinational organizations, savvy small and midsize businesses are now realizing that they, too, can extend their remote hiring offshore, a strategy I'll explain in the very next chapter.

CHAPTER 7

Why Offshore Talent Is No Longer Optional for Most Small and Midsize Businesses

---

"The secret to my success is that we've gone to exceptional lengths to hire the best people in the world."

– Steve Jobs

Opening your organization to the potential of remote talent unlocks many benefits for your business. However, you can access even more high performers by expanding your remote talent pool from around the globe.

Making this decision will soon be unavoidable for most small and midsize businesses. Why? First, great talent is more essential today to reaching your goals than it ever has been. Second, the talent you need is harder than ever to find locally. And third, financial pressures—such as rising salary costs and shrinking margins—make it imperative to think differently about where and how you source talent.

In this chapter, I will take you through recognizing when to expand your talent search to offshore markets. I'll reveal the three major considerations you'll want to work through before you offshore any of your remote roles, and I'll show you exactly how you can successfully source top talent from other countries, even if it's a new experience for you.

Why Offshore Now?

You already know you need to look far and wide to find great talent. Yet small and midsize businesses are finding that even opening up their roles to be fully remote doesn't allow them to find the talent they want within the domestic talent pool.

In the U.S., talent shortages are a nationwide issue. Going remote does allow you to reach out to more people, but you're still facing a competition for talent that's as fierce—if not fiercer—than the competition for customers. 2024 marked a year in which labor force participation rates *fell*, leaving you with fewer workers available for every open job. Plus, as we've touched on before, more than 10,000 Baby Boomers exit the workforce *each day*, and some of those who remain have less-than-needed attitudes and work ethics. You need people with a great attitude and work ethic, along with skill sets that are dramatically different from those of the generations before them.

It adds up to a perfect storm of talent troubles for small and midsize businesses, where every seat counts and each hire needs to be exceptional. There are workers available to hire... but fewer overall than there used to be. Then, thanks to generational attitude shifts and changes in the culture around preparing for work, the existing domestic talent pool is packed with people who might not share your work ethic and habits.

You can feel this domestic talent tap out first-hand when you post a role but are underwhelmed by the applicants, or when you seem to only be attracting talent that would be a poor cultural fit for your organization. In addition, salary demands can be excessive, or you may find that new hires' expectations for advancement and compensation don't match their skill levels.

The reality is that plenty of very talented, highly skilled, and extremely motivated and engaged workers are available around the world. Many of them have excellent English skills—at least as good and occasionally even better English, in fact, than some domestic workers. They often have stellar experience and are hungry to put their work skills to good use. The attitudes, engagement, and productivity levels they bring to the table are at the top of the charts. Plus, living in countries with a lower cost of living means their salary demands are lower. An analysis by Embarca comparing U.S. and Latin American compensation for roles like customer support and marketing found that LATAM salaries are typically 16% to 43% of U.S. salaries. At WBN, we know this firsthand. Around 80% of our team, including key members of our leadership team, is based in Latin America.

This can help get you your dream team, as many, including my company and hundreds of our clients, are experiencing. You can often get top-quality talent in less time, at a lower cost, and with less stress, by expanding your remote roles overseas.

High-Performing Talent for Key Roles

Even better? Your dream team of performers can often include more team members. Due to the lower cost of living and lower salary requirements of offshore talent, small and midsize businesses often have the chance to fill roles that are important to the company but which would be cost prohibitive to fill domestically.

These roles can range from departmental assistants to things like fleet safety coordinators. The impact of adding this staff can be monumental. For example, Peter Morandi, CEO at Eastman Cooke Construction in New York, hired an assistant (located in Latin America) for the estimating department. An on-site assistant would have been prohibitively expensive, but his new remote assistant enables that department to get much more work done while allowing the in-house estimators to focus on higher-value tasks.

In another case, Larry Zogby (CEO, RDS Same Day Delivery in NY), had always wanted someone to work with his drivers on safety, but it was cost prohibitive. By looking offshore, he was able to hire a logistics safety manager who meets with drivers over Zoom to go over the reports from their driver tracking software on their phones. Accidents are down, as are insurance premiums.

Safety is just one example of a role that is easily managed remotely or offshore today. Businesses are increasingly filling a wide variety of roles using offshore talent, including:

Administrative Support	Accounting Services
IT Services	Digital Marketing
Software Development	Human Resources
Customer Support	Content Writing
Graphic Design	Video Production and Animation
Financial Analysis	Project Management
Data Entry	Technical Support
Product Design	Mechanical Engineering
Payroll Management	Quality Assurance Testing
Market Research	Legal Support

This list isn't exhaustive, but it shows how strategic offshore hiring can be—far beyond administrative or customer service roles.

Three Key Considerations When Deciding Which Regions to Use for Your Offshore Talent Source

As you look offshore, not all talent locations are going to be equally useful to you. Here, I will take you through three key elements to keep in mind so that you can match with good talent that will be easy to integrate into your regular operations. While our focus at WBN is Latin America—other areas like Asia (predominantly the Philippines), Eastern Europe, parts of Africa, and even countries like Portugal can be excellent offshore talent sources.

Consideration #1: Do you need time zone alignment or a complementary time zone?

Time zone alignment refers to whether your remote team keeps the same office hours as you. They may be doing that because they share your time zone, as Latin American nations do with most of the U.S., or because they're willing to work to your schedule, as you might see with workers in the Philippines or India who may choose to essentially work the night shift to match up with you. Now, I feel strongly that people should be sleeping during their natural night, but I do understand that for a great opportunity, international talent may be willing to redesign their lives around your preferred normal business hours, and some business owners might be okay with this.

For some companies—and especially companies that run around the clock or have 24/7 customer service expectations—complementary time zones can be a huge advantage. Instead of trying to run U.S. workers all night, you can have a team that works during their normal daylight hours on your behalf. I've seen this done in stages, too, where a U.S. team works to East Coast business hours, an Asian team covers U.S. evenings into the night, and a European team covers extreme early morning into mid-day. It keeps everyone on their normal sleep cycle but gives excellent round-the-clock coverage. In other cases, such as companies with work that doesn't need to be done contemporaneously, time zone differences don't need to be a major factor in your hiring decision, allowing you to focus on getting the skilled players you need.

Consideration #2: What is the level of English proficiency needed?

English language proficiency is important for international talent. You need them to be able to communicate and understand well in English. However, it is very beneficial to divide proficiency needs between written and verbal.

Verbal skills refer to basic fluency in the language, but also much more than just pure fluency. It can describe how skilled a candidate is at calming difficult customers or making (or assisting in) sales presentations, and how polished they come across in different work and social settings. It captures a level of comfort and talent in verbal communication that can be essential in many roles.

On the other hand, written language skills can be greatly enhanced with AI tools. English writing is frequently leveled up with technology programs, such as Grammarly or ChatGPT editors. While I have seen domestic employees use these tools, international staff tend to use them more.

For example, if you want this talent to be in customer-facing roles and talk with your customers or your team on a regular basis, they need excellent verbal skills. Same for executive assistants, vendor management roles, or project managers. They should be able to speak clearly in a professional conversational manner, with an accent level that doesn't interfere with the ability to be understood clearly. On the other hand, if there's no customer interaction or the role isn't verbally based (i.e., data analysis or text-based IT support), then written English will be enough, and the level of their accent isn't going to matter much. There are a number of AI and tech tools to help you expand your prospect pool.

As you consider fluency needs with regard to where you might look for talent, both Latin America and certain countries in Asia offer talent pools with strong English language skills. While proficiency levels are generally high in both regions, the accents can differ. In Asia, particularly in the Philippines, English has been an official language of business and fine arts since the 1920s, resulting in a more neutral, American-influenced accent. The country also ranks 2nd in Asia (just behind Singapore) in the EF English Proficiency Index.

In Latin America, proximity to the U.S. and business opportunities have led to widespread English education, with many students fluent in both Spanish and English by the time they finish high school. However, the accent is typically more Latin-influenced. Ultimately, the choice may come down to which accent aligns best with your business needs and preferences.

Consideration #3: How important are cultural similarities?

A final consideration is the cultural similarities between where you're based and where your international talent is based. This may be something important to you, or it may not be, in terms of how your remote talent will connect with your existing staff and your client base.

For example, in Latin America, there's a similarity in culture and values with North America. In Asia, it can be very different, with values and a historical culture very different from dominant North American norms. Depending on the degree to which the role you are hiring for is interacting with clients, vendors, and other team members, and what kind of rapport you'd like built in those interactions, these things may matter differently to your firm.

How to Successfully Source Talent from Other Countries

Once you've made the decision to internationalize your talent pool, the first question is usually, "How exactly am I supposed to do that?" Let me walk you through it and let you know what you'd need to do for a DIY solution and what your options are for outsourcing the task.

Now, you may have already dipped your toes in international waters with companies like Upwork, 99 Designs, or Fiverr. There, you have a chance to see what international talent can do in a limited-scope project capacity. The screening, matching, and project management are almost gamified compared to real life. While it gives you a taste of the talent and efficiency available abroad, often, those you'll meet on those platforms are freelancers who may not be at all representative of the commitment, energy, and engagement available to you through a direct, full-time hire.

When it comes to hiring overseas talent directly, you'll find that many of the same tools you'd use for domestic remote hiring can also be used internationally. You can put jobs on LinkedIn and take resumes and applications online from all over the world, or just specific countries and geographic areas. You can run your own vetting and screening process to narrow down your choices. Just as in the U.S., assessments, if you use them, can be delivered through online platforms, interviews can be conducted with Zoom, and offers can be made and signed via DocuSign or even Dropbox systems. From a payroll perspective, there are companies like Deel that specialize in offshore payroll and compliance. There's a lot of flexibility and a lot of options, and as long as you're willing to take charge of the details and spend the time, there's no reason you can't see it through from start to finish yourself. Though many small and midsize businesses aren't great at hiring, if it's a strength of yours, by all means, lean in!

Alternatively, you can outsource the process to a talent provider. WBN is a great talent provider (I'm biased), and there are many others. You want to partner with someone who has established processes in place for presenting great candidates easily and quickly.

If you decide that you want to tap into a talent provider, here are questions to ask them. Use those that are appropriate for your needs.

Checklist Questions for Vetting Talent Providers

1. What is the process to rigorously evaluate candidates?

2. How are candidates tested on advanced communication skills, including English proficiency?

3. How competitive is the selection process? What percentage of candidates are accepted? (e.g., At WBN, only the top 1-3% of candidates that apply qualify to be presented to our clients).

4. How have candidates been tested on skills tailored to the specific job role (e.g., executive assistants, project managers)? How do they ensure that the talent has significant relevant experience?

5. Does the company perform reference and criminal background checks?

6. How are candidates assessed for communication, organizational, and adaptability skills?

7. What in-depth consultations happen with your business to understand your unique hiring needs, including company culture, role goals, and personality fit? Does the company provide guidance to help you identify the right traits and skills for your hires?

8. Are candidates tailor-matched to the role based on both hard and soft skills?

9. To what extent do candidates buy into each opportunity prior to an interview with potential clients?

10. What is their process to communicate with clients and talent after hiring to ensure satisfaction and alignment?

11. Do they offer guarantees, such as a replacement if the hire isn't a fit? Do they lock you in with long-term contracts?

12. Does the company have proven results and positive feedback from both clients and placed talent?

By asking these questions, you can evaluate talent provider options and choose the partner that's best for your needs. (See Appendix C for WorkBetterNow's response to these questions.)

Great Talent, Better Margins

With approximately 80% of our team based in Latin America, WBN is first-hand proof, along with 250+ clients, that you can build a great team with offshore talent... while *improving* your margins.

As I write this in early 2025, we are at an inflection point where small and midsize businesses hiring overseas talent is no longer "weird" or the exception but is becoming the norm. Going international can help you staff quickly, find top talent at very attractive price points, and expand your capabilities without needing to carry the cost of a larger physical presence. You can do it yourself or lean on a company like WBN to get you great talent and handle 95% of the hiring process.

What's the best role to start with on this? In the bonus resources at the end of this book, I'll show you the perfect "test run" position to try and reveal how even offshoring this single role can have a dramatic positive impact on you and your organization.

In the meantime, there's something else brewing in the talent world that you can't afford to overlook. It's how AI and automation are reshaping the speed, power, and productivity of your talent, which we'll explore in our next chapter together.

CHAPTER 8

How AI and Automation Will Help You Mitigate the Talent Crisis

"By the end of the decade, there will be two kinds of companies. Those who utilize AI and those who are out of business."

– Peter Diamandis

With past technological innovations, companies could take a bit of a "wait and see" approach to adoption. When the commercial Internet arrived, it seeped out into the broader business world over the next decade. Social media took years to catch on as a business concept. Even automation, which has existed for some time, has only been widely integrated into small and midsize business software tools in the last five to ten years.

The arrival of AI has marked a turning point. Adoption has been fast and near-universal, especially for small and midsize businesses. According to a September 2024 survey by The U.S. Chamber of Commerce and Teneo, nearly every small business—98%—said they are using AI in some form or a tool enabled by AI.[14] I'm extremely happy to see that, and I hope this chapter shows you even more ways to level up with AI as well as automation.

AI and automation tools are a gift to small and midsize businesses. They can help you mitigate the pain of the talent crisis, and they can help you upskill and expand the capabilities of your organization. Here, I'll look briefly at each in turn and how they can connect to your larger talent journey and performance goals.

Get the Team Involved

When AI first came out, in the form of those early ChatGPT models, I knew two things. One, this was something that would fundamentally impact our business and our clients' businesses. Two, I wouldn't be the one at my company figuring out how.

Why not? After all, I am pretty good with tech. However, as a GenXer, I remember rotary phones and the world before the Internet. The online world and the digital environment are not my native space. For many of my team members, though, AI is just the latest cool toy to arrive in their digital playground. They've grown up in a digitally assisted world already, and their status as digital natives gives them a comfort that any smart business owner can leverage.

So, at WBN, and what I recommend you do as well, I've made experimenting with AI tools to expand our capabilities something everyone is tasked with doing. After all, when AI arrived on the scene, my partner Andrew and I recognized that we were the oldest members of the organization. We knew that some members of our team, being younger and more digitally-native than we were, would figure out how to use AI more quickly and effectively than we would. So, we asked them to start experimenting and playing around with it, and they then got their teams on board with running tests, trying out new tools, and sharing what they'd found.

Now that our team is getting comfortable with AI, we're focused on systematically incorporating AI into our workflows—using it to assist team members with their responsibilities and streamline processes across the organization.

AI Expands Your Organizational Capabilities

The big lesson for us has been how AI can expand our organizational capabilities. It will be the same for you, too.

Small and midsize businesses simply can't afford to spend days doing what AI tools can perform in minutes. Your smartest humans need to be aligned against your strategic priorities and highest value relationship opportunities—and your smartest AI tools need to be set up to support the rest.

What are some of the most successful things we've discovered and implemented? I'll give you our current favorites, though this list changes frequently thanks to our ongoing trials and tests.

- **AI Edit & Polish:** We use AI to edit emails and other communications to make them more professional.

- **AI Note-taking:** Multiple departments use AI note-taking tools, freeing up our human minds to be fully present in sales conversations, interviews, and client interactions. It also allows us to provide continuous feedback based on notes and end our calls with automatically created to-do and follow-up lists.

- **AI-Driven Candidate Matching:** We use AI to analyze client-provided job descriptions and match them to candidates from our talent pool, ensuring precision in selecting the best fit. The AI tool supports the recruiter, as the recruiter is still running the process, but AI helps to reduce natural human bias.

- **AI Voice Interviews:** We are testing AI-based voice interviews with candidates (in addition to human-based interviews) to measure their engagement levels.

- **AI-Prompted Process Improvements:** We have processes for everything in the company, and we use AI to both create new processes and improve existing processes.

- **Enhanced Predictive Analytics:** We use AI tools to forecast future hiring needs based on historical data and industry trends.

- **Brainstorming Partner:** Many of us, including me, use AI as a thought partner to get "feedback" on new ideas.

We plan to expand our use of AI across every department and enhance training to ensure WorkBetterNow Certified Professionals™ are "AI-enabled" for our clients. This is just the beginning.

Automation Eases the Workload

No human worker likes repetitive, time-consuming work. Automations have been a real godsend in this area, allowing repetitive tasks to be the computer or algorithm's job instead of requiring additional headcount. This gets your valuable humans out of some of the drudgery so that they can be more innovative and strategic in their output. Plus, your business can enjoy some of the other benefits of automation, like fewer errors and faster cycle times, which can unlock better customer experiences, improved employee experiences, and better overall efficiency and margins.

Some of our favorite types of automation are the ones that shave hours off tasks and help those tasks be performed to a higher standard. Data migrations and imports are a prime example, as automation can prevent transfer errors while saving tons of human time. Tools that allow software systems to speak to each other without human input also reduce errors internally and with customer-facing operations. This improves everyone's experience and frees up your team to focus on higher-value tasks.

To give you a few real-world examples, here are some of the ways WBN is currently using automation:

- **Payroll Automation:** We streamline the payroll processing of our WBN Certified Professionals™ by leveraging CRM data, ensuring accuracy and reducing administrative burden.

- **Smart Applicant Screening:** This accelerates the initial recruitment process, allowing our recruiters to focus on qualified candidates while providing faster responses to applicants.

- **Cross-System Synchronization:** This seamlessly integrates our applicant tracking system (ATS) and CRM systems, eliminating manual data transfer and ensuring consistent information across platforms.

- **Digital Document Workflow:** This automates document generation and triggers relevant actions in the CRM upon signature, streamlining administrative processes and improving tracking.

- **Automated Customer Feedback:** We use this to systematically collect insights from new customers, enabling continuous improvement and identifying upselling opportunities for future campaigns.

We add more automations as we discover uses for them. Given the benefits, automation will continue to be a major part of our workflows as we continue to aggressively grow and expand our business.

Don't Get Left Behind

Technologies like automation and AI can help you mitigate the talent crisis. They can help you grow with fewer headcount additions (and yes, some companies are already reducing their headcount with these technologies). They also improve efficiency, effectiveness, and both customer and employee experiences. And the pace of change here is extraordinary—AI is improving by the day. New AI agents, which will soon be able to handle complex, multi-step processes with little oversight, are quickly moving from concept to reality.

At WBN, we now require department heads to re-evaluate how automation and AI can be implemented before making a new hire. We want new hires to add and expand on our capabilities; not duplicate the work of tools we already have at our fingertips. This ensures that every system—and every person—is operating in their own zone of maximum potential.

Easy to use and inexpensive, automation is within reach for every business. AI is now driving the biggest transformation in business in our lifetimes. Whether you start slowly or dive in headfirst, the important thing is to *get started* and build AI into your business DNA before you're left behind.

Not sure where to start? Ask AI.

Building Your Dream Today

"The real competitive advantage in any business is one word only, which is 'people.'"
– Kamil Toume

Throughout this book, you've heard me beat the same drum: talent, talent, talent.

Great talent is the foundation of every thriving business. With the right people in the right seats, you can run your company with energy, clarity, and momentum. You'll no longer be stuck fighting fires or working endless hours just to hold things together. Instead, you get to lead, innovate, and grow while your competitors wonder how you're pulling so far ahead.

That's the power of building your Dream Team. And even in today's challenging talent market, you can do it. This book has shown you how to find outstanding people, set them up for success, and create the culture that keeps them motivated and engaged.

Of course, results don't come from knowledge alone—they come from action. Leverage the resources in this book, and you'll have everything you need to put your company on the path to lasting success.

You Deserve a Better Future—One Powered by Great Talent

Imagine what it would be like to have outstanding help on your side. No more feeling shorthanded or having to clean up after continual underperformers. Instead, you can focus on what you do best and most enjoy doing, all the while surrounded by a team that enthusiastically and actively seeks to live your mission and grow your company.

Great talent will spot problems early and solve them without you needing to get into the details. They'll bring ideas forward for product improvements and ways to expand your offerings and business relationships. Above all, they'll ensure that every client and business partner who works with you comes away impressed by what you do and how you do it.

You will—perhaps for the first time—be able to truly focus yourself on achieving your business and growth goals. Unshackled from talent woes, you will be able to push forward in ways that will make it fun again to run your business and bring to life all the hopes you had when you became a business owner.

Build Your Dream Team—Starting Today

As the talent conversation intensifies, you'll hear more and more about shortages, struggles, and challenges. But here's the truth: you don't have to live in crisis mode. You can flip the script and create something far more powerful—your Dream Team.

I've been in your shoes, and I've also experienced what it's like on the other side: running a business where the right people are in the right seats, aligned with the mission, and driving growth in ways you never thought possible. And I can 100% tell you—the effort you put into building your Dream Team pays off far beyond your expectations.

This book, along with the bonus resources I've prepared, is your playbook for doing exactly that. You can keep struggling with underperformers and short-staffed teams—or you can take action to attract, build, and retain the Dream Team that will carry your business forward.

Everything comes back to talent and culture. Every success flows from there. If you make talent your priority and pull in the world's top remote nearshore professionals, you'll not only escape today's challenges—you'll unlock the freedom, growth, and fulfillment you imagined when you first became a business owner.

Your Dream Team is waiting.

Why Every Business Owner Must Have An Assistant

"If you don't have an assistant, you are an assistant."
– Jack Daly

The book you've just read was dedicated to helping you build a dream team for greater operational efficiency, better profit margins, and the potential to achieve your business goals. As a part of that, in Chapter 7, I promised to show you the perfect "test run" to illustrate how even offshoring a single role could have a dramatic positive impact on you and your organization. This section offers you that guidance, and I hope you find it to be a practical and useful tool.

Hiring an executive assistant was one of the most important decisions I've ever made to improve my business and my life.

Here's why: As a business owner, it can feel like there are never enough hours in the day. You have a million different priorities while managing a rapidly changing business. Your business depends on you to show up and execute from a position of full executive capacity. You have your day-to-day tasks (including the many fires that pop up) and the strategic work that also needs to get done. Your unique skill set, executive vision, and leadership abilities set the tone and direction for everyone and everything else.

This is why it is incredibly limiting—not just to you but to your entire organization—for you to be doing administrative tasks. Now I get it—you're the owner, and it can be very hard to let go of certain tasks, especially if you have doubts about anyone else being able to get them done to the standards you expect. Also, even if you wanted to offload some of the admin on your plate, having the time to bring someone in and train them to do those things can seem too much of a burden.

Yet, given the long list of critical, high-level issues that owners face today—including the pace of change in the business world and the level of competition—having an assistant is no longer optional.

Right here, right now, I'm going to show you how to unlock the value of an executive assistant. You'll see the real value of the time you can reclaim. Plus, I will share my top tactics for effectively managing an assistant, including a robust list of tasks you can shift over to your assistant's plate for good.

Why Being Able to Stay in Your Zone of Genius Matters So Much to Your Productivity and Bottom Line

Your effectiveness as a business leader depends on your ability to spend the bulk of your time on strategic issues and working within your zone of genius. Your zone of genius lies at the intersection of what you do best and what drives value. The more time you can spend within your genius zone, the more you can accomplish. You should spend 80% of your time in this zone. However, most are lucky to spend 20% here.

To give a brief example from my own life, my zone of genius is understanding small and midsize businesses and coming up with solutions for them. When I'm operating in that space, I'm spending more time with customers to better understand how we can help them, and unlocking new opportunities for partnerships and joint ventures (plus finding time to write a book!) The more I have let go and let others do work outside my unique ability, the more our business has grown. My energy is high, my mood is great, and I'm making a difference in the world around me.

Most business owners have similar "zones of genius"—the high-payoff activities where their unique contribution creates an outsized impact. These usually include things like building key relationships, working on big deals, refining strategy to keep up with the pace of change, mentoring your leadership team, and making the big calls only you can make. When you're in this zone, you multiply the value of your time and position your business for long-term success.

By contrast, low-payoff activities—administrative tasks, operational details, routine scheduling, or troubleshooting—don't require your unique skills and drain both your energy and your potential impact. These are the tasks that should be delegated to an assistant or to other members of your team. Every minute you spend on them is a minute stolen from the high-payoff work that drives growth and keeps you ahead of the curve.

I don't light up over operational details, and my strength isn't in execution. It may be different for you, but for me, time spent in those areas or on those tasks subtracts from my potential for impact and achievement in my business. Every minute I spend on that kind of work actually creates risk for my business.

As discussed throughout the book, the pace of change in the business world is ever-increasing. You have to be able to keep pace and adapt, or you risk falling behind, pulled down by tasks that shouldn't be on your plate in the first place. That's the tough reality we all live in. Yet, until I got serious about offloading those things outside my genius zone, I could never escape those shackles, and I know it's the same for many other business executives and entrepreneurs.

What a Typical Day Looks Like for the Average Executive

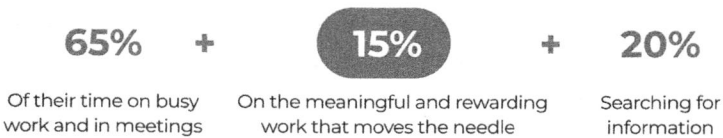

65%	+	15%	+	20%
Of their time on busy work and in meetings		On the meaningful and rewarding work that moves the needle		Searching for information

This is an equation that needs to change. You need to be able to spend less time on tasks like travel arrangements, invoicing, and scheduling, and more time on things like strategic planning, competitor analysis, and new product development. Indeed, successful owners spend as much as 80% of their time in their zone of genius.

It is possible to get there. When we built WBN, we built it with a team to handle the administrative tasks right from the start. This means that these days, I mostly work in my unique ability zone, and I have time to speak, travel, spend time with my family, and even get in time to play my guitar. My business partner, Andrew, will tell you that when I am doing this— working in my zone of genius—I am making a much bigger impact on the company (and we are both less cranky).

For WBN clients we've provided with assistants, the impact is similar. They rave to us about reclaiming their days, having more time and energy for strategic work and client connection, and minimizing unwanted interruptions. As a result, we're seeing dramatic bottom-line growth and clients enjoying freedom and a return to sanity after years—decades at times—of being their company's non-stop workhorses.

The Value You Gain by Leveraging an Assistant

With an assistant, you can't simply look at the cost. You also need to consider the value of making the investment. To help with that, here's a look at the amount you effectively pay when you do administrative work yourself.

Annual comp >	$200,000	$400,000	$600,000
Hourly Rate	$100	$200	$300
$ Spent on admin work (weekly*)	$2,000	$4,000	$6,000
$ Spent on admin work (yearly*)	$100,000	$200,000	$300,000

*assumes 20hr/weeks spent on admin tasks.

Suppose you spend as little as 50% of your time on administrative activities—which sounds like a lot but is still below the typical executive's average—and your compensation (including any non-tax related distributions) is $200,000. In that case, that means you're spending nearly $100,000 a year on administrative work. *Moreover, imagine what you would do with an additional 20 hours per week (or 4 hours per day).*

I think it's clear by now that the easiest way to start increasing the time you have available for strategic, meaningful work is to have an assistant take all the administrative assignments off your plate. Yet, what kinds of things can a remote executive assistant do for you?

The answer is a lot more than you think—plus dozens of tasks you'd never imagine until you have someone in place actively looking for ways to make your life easier. Here's another way to look at it: if your time is worth $100 to $300 an hour, why are you spending it on $25-an-hour work? Every hour you spend on admin is an hour you're not spending on growth, strategy, or leadership—the things only you can do. Bringing on an assistant positions you to lead more strategically and frees you to focus on high-impact work.

The Part-Time Option is a Mistake

Now, many business owners think they'll toe-dip into the world of having an assistant. They don't need that much help… they just want to try it… so they try to pick up a part-time assistant. It rarely goes as planned, and I don't advocate for that approach. If you're willing to admit that you could use a little help, the reality is that you could benefit from a lot of help, and you probably have more than enough on your plate to keep an assistant busy full-time.

Further, we've found over the years that hiring part-time assistants is an unstable setup for most business owners. There are markedly higher turnover rates, which are incredibly disruptive and limit your ability to rely on your assistant to be there for you. Plus, most part-time assistants serve multiple clients, which can reduce their overall efficiency and attention to detail in your business.

Additionally, there's no denying that someone who is wholly focused on you and deeply understands the rhythms of your day and your business life will be able to start anticipating what you need before you even have to ask. They'll be able to be more efficient and a better performer for you, exclusively, than they would be if they were split with someone else or shared within a business unit. And they are there when you need them.

How to Get the Most Out of Your Executive Assistant

Now that the business case for an executive assistant is clear, it's time to look at what tasks to give them and how to get the most from them.

I counsel executives hiring an assistant for the first time that you don't need to have everything figured out the moment they arrive. You want to put together a starting slate of tasks and then lean into the evolution. It may be that your assistant can handle everything you have, plus assist with marketing or other operational functions in your business. It may be that your needs were greater than you imagined they were. That's okay. It's a process, and the best assistants will help you figure it out.

What to Do *Before* You Hire Your First Assistant

As you prepare to hire your first assistant, you'll want to spend a little time thinking about two things. The first is what you'll do with the time they'll free up for you, and the second is what you'd like them to do for you.

Your first step is to reflect on what you will do with an additional 10-15 hours/week (2-3 hours a day) of productive time. Make a list. Is this when you could finally visit that potential new business partner's location? Is this when you could start the new service offering development you've been putting off? Could you take on an additional consulting client or accept an additional production contract? Where would your business benefit the most from consistent additional attention from you? It's powerful to get this down on paper… After all, you have been doing admin-related work for so long, you may no longer fully appreciate the true potential of your own additional time.

Next, plan what your assistant will do. It's okay not to be 100% sure. You've been doing a lot of this admin work yourself for a long time, and it can be hard to pull back and reflect on what can be taken off your plate. So, at WBN, we've created a simple activity you can do to help you develop your first job description and initial set of tasks. We call it the "3-day task list," and it's something we do with all new clients as they prepare to bring on their first assistant.

Basically, for three days, write down everything that you do. Then, look over your list and identify everything that can be delegated. This provides a good starting point of responsibilities and a framework for the job description for your ideal assistant. We've also found that many people who do this are surprised at how many tasks they do that could be handed to a reliable assistant.

Onboarding Your Assistant

During the initial onboarding phase, you want to establish a solid foundation by defining tasks, fostering clear communication, introducing tools, building rapport, and providing comprehensive instructions (as with any remote team member, communicate early and often with your assistant, especially in your initial weeks together).

1. Clearly outline your goals, tasks, and responsibilities for your assistant. Use your 3-day task list to provide a starting list for your assistant.

2. Discuss your timeline and process for adding new tasks to the list.

3. If you do not have written processes for items on your task list, don't worry. Explain the end results you'd like to see and any other relevant details, and then have your assistant handle the documentation of processes. Then, they can refer back to it and share it with others when they are on PTO or when you are onboarding a new employee.

4. Establish regular check-ins to discuss expectations, answer questions, and provide guidance. Create an environment where your assistant feels comfortable seeking clarification, just as you would for any other remote talent on your team.

5. Go over the tools and platforms you'll use for communication, task management, and document sharing. Provide training or resources if needed.

6. Dedicate time to educate your assistant on your preferred working style. When a task is not done to

your liking, address the root cause, not just the task at hand.

7. Clearly communicate deadlines, quality standards, and specific instructions for tasks. Providing comprehensive guidelines ensures accurate outcomes. And don't hesitate to tell them about the things that you don't like (e.g., sloppy mistakes, missed deadlines, etc).

Speaking from experience, while you will benefit from giving your assistant more information and responsibilities from the beginning, don't stress over it. It took me time to get comfortable giving credit card numbers and access to some documents to my assistants. Once I did,

I did wish I had done it sooner, but that's a place of trust you'll need to get to on your own timetable.

Ongoing Management

Once you have your assistant in the role, you'll want to manage them intelligently to ensure the continued success of the relationship. Now, this isn't something to stress over, though I know many first-timers with an assistant do worry about the management aspects. Capable assistants largely manage themselves and require minimal touch from you to stay on track and deliver above and beyond expectations.

1. Encourage your assistant to take proactive steps, offer suggestions, and contribute ideas for improvement. Encouraging autonomy enhances creativity and

independent problem-solving. Remember, the more they can take off your plate, the more time you'll have to spend on the tasks you truly enjoy and the work that truly matters.

2. Maintain regular communication channels for updates, questions, and feedback. Address any concerns promptly to maintain a smooth workflow. Figure out a system where your assistant is regularly (every day/every other day) communicating what is on their "pending list" so that you don't have to continually ask.

3. Offer both positive feedback for accomplishments and constructive feedback for improvements. Having regular feedback sessions on the calendar will take the pressure off these conversations and contribute to ongoing growth, as well as allow you to keep tabs on the effectiveness of your collaboration and any needed adjustments.

4. Embrace flexibility and be open to changes as you settle into a productive rhythm as a team. This will allow you to continue to improve your processes back and forth.

5. Support your assistant's professional growth by offering learning opportunities and exposure to new tasks. Some assistants love that role and make a good life-long career out of it. Others who start as assistants choose to transition into other roles and can grow into trusted

lieutenants or directors within your organization with the right training and opportunities.

Some clients even find that their assistants become excellent examples to other departments within their organizations. Once it is clear how much having a good assistant helps you, other departments may campaign to get their own. Other firms, including WBN, have found assistants for sales departments and marketing groups to be extremely beneficial.

Closing Thoughts

Your business depends on you being able to spend as much time as possible within your zone of genius. This is what allows you to grow, expand, and scale your business. Staying bogged down and distracted with administrative work limits your success, and that's a limit you can remove by bringing in a dedicated remote executive assistant.

Assistants can unlock incredible value for you at a price point that's extremely attractive compared to the ongoing costs of doing the work yourself. By being smart with your onboarding, using best practices for ongoing management, and being open to supporting your assistant into other roles of trust and authority within your organization, you can maximize the value of your investment.

How WBN Helps Companies Running EOS

When WBN switched to running on EOS (Entrepreneurial Operating System) four years ago, it was a game changer for our company. Between being 100% remote (with 80% of our team in Latin America) and our aggressive growth levels, we needed the performance metrics and management frameworks of EOS to keep our company focused on doing the right things in the right ways. This helped us make #114 on the 2024 Inc. 5000 list and win a 2024 Power Partner Award, key external recognition of how EOS was helping our organization outperform.

As we implemented and continued with EOS, however, I also began to see how the unique services that our company provides could help bring the full potential of the EOS approach to life in other firms. In particular, WBN helps companies with the "People" component of EOS. Providing affordable, high-quality remote talent (WBN Certified Professionals™) directly addresses the Right People, Right Seats (RPRS) principle, and it helps improve team culture and values alignment, and allows business owners to do more of the Delegate & Elevate behaviors to unlock maximum performance.

How WBN Helps EOS Companies with the People Component

Our strength at WBN is combing through thousands of resumes each month to uncover the best nearshore talent -- and we're extremely thorough. Our TopTalentFilter™ results in only 1- 3% of applicants each month moving forward in our process, and an even smaller percentage passing through our final screening systems and presented to clients. It's a lot of work, but we're proud of our skill in uncovering amazing talent.

What we do feeds directly into the EOS focus on RPRS. When a business comes to us with a need, we match them, via our PrecisionMatch™ process, with 3 WBN Certified Professional™ candidates for the business to interview. Each of these candidates meets the EOS GWC standard (gets it, wants it, and has the capacity to do it). The business then selects the best of these matched candidates.

Many of our clients -- as we did when we adopted EOS for WBN itself -- also utilize the Delegate & Elevate principle. We provide the talent, and EOS provides the framework for them to hand off tasks to our capable team members, which gives them the freedom to tackle the bigger-picture responsibilities and continue to grow their organizations.

"My experience with WBN has been fantastic. Despite being in different countries, there's a level of trust that makes WBN professionals a true component of our organization... When we hand them a process, we're confident it'll be executed flawlessly, times a thousand. They've become the backbone of our business."
— Andrew Schenkel, CEO of Double Play Marketing and Sales, on running EOS with WBN talent

Driving Operational Performance with WBN and EOS

Of course, it's not just about using WBN to fill roles. When combined with EOS frameworks, WBN talent can also help address underlying operational issues that might be holding your business back.

Consider this example from EOS implementer Philip Pfeifer, who worked with a client struggling to hit their sales and marketing targets. The client was already a WBN customer, having previously hired a remote executive assistant through WBN. But despite having strong people in Marketing and Sales, they kept missing their goals.

As Philip and his client dug into the problem, they discovered that the real problem was in Operations. The department was understaffed, and Marketing and Sales kept getting pulled into Operations for various operational issues related to delivery and customer service. It was the Operations team that had RPRS issues, which were being back-filled by Marketing and Sales, masking the true source of the problem.

The good news? Once the issue had been identified, Philip's client staffed up in Operations with a WorkBetterNow Certified Professional™. This solved the personnel issues and freed up their growth team to focus on their core tasks. Stagnation went out the window, and the company is now bringing on new clients at their new, higher fees, and doing a better job of competing and winning new bids from competitors.

How Will WBN Help Your Business?

EOS principles help businesses with clarity, alignment, and traction. Yet, all of those aspects are powered by people. At WBN, people are our specialty, and we deeply understand and appreciate the impact of the EOS approach. We've seen first-hand what the combination of our talent and the EOS system can deliver.

WBN's Responses to Talent Provider Vetting Questions (As Found in Chapter 7)

1. **What is the process to rigorously evaluate candidates?**
Using our TopTalentFilter,™ WBN screens thousands of applicants monthly through a multi-stage process including multiple interviews, communication and English assessments, role-specific skills tests, and comprehensive background and reference checks.

2. **How are candidates tested on advanced communication skills, including English proficiency?**
Candidates undergo structured interviews, written exercises, and real-time problem-solving tasks in English to assess fluency, clarity, and comprehension.

3. **How competitive is the selection process? What percentage of candidates are accepted?**
Only the top **1–3%** of applicants make it through the TopTalentFilter and qualify to become WBN Certified Professionals™ (CPs).

4. **Have candidates been tested on skills tailored to the specific job role? How do they ensure that the talent has significant relevant experience?**
   Role-specific evaluation includes a review of past work experience, scenario-based exercises, and verification of a proven track record in similar positions.

5. **Does the company perform reference and criminal background checks?**
   Yes. All candidates undergo three professional reference checks and must provide a criminal record from their local national security entity before being presented to clients.

6. **How are candidates assessed for communication, organizational, and adaptability skills?**
   WBN uses structured interviews, scenario-based challenges, and targeted skills testing to evaluate each candidate's ability to thrive in the workplace.

7. **What in-depth consultations happen with your business to understand your unique hiring needs, including company culture, role goals, and personality fit? Does the company provide guidance to help you identify the right traits and skills for your hires?**
   Each prospective client has a consultation with a WBN Client Consultant to define goals, culture, role requirements, and working style preferences.

8. **Are candidates tailor-matched to the role based on both hard and soft skills?**
   Yes. Using our PrecisionMatch™ process candidates are matched to client needs based on technical expertise, soft skills, and culture fit to ensure effective contributions from day one.

9. **To what extent do candidates buy into each opportunity prior to an interview with potential clients?**
   Qualified WBN Certified Professionals™ opt in to roles they're interested in. Fit and interest are confirmed on both sides, and only aligned candidates move forward.

10. **What is their process to communicate with clients and talent after hiring to ensure satisfaction and alignment?**
    WBN's Talent Partners and Talent Coordinators maintain ongoing communication with both the client and WBN Certified Professional™ to monitor performance and proactively address any issues that arise.

11. **Do they offer guarantees, such as a replacement if the hire isn't a fit? Do they lock you in with long-term contracts?**
    While it doesn't happen often, WBN replaces WBN Certified Professionals™. In addition, there are no long-term contracts.

12. **Does the company have proven results and positive feedback from both clients and placed talent?**
    WBN has a strong record of long-term relationships, repeat business, and positive feedback from both clients and placed professionals.

Additional Resources

The strategies in The New Talent Playbook are just the beginning. To help you put them into action, we've created a set of resources designed to make your next step easier.

Scan the QR code or visit thenewtalentplaybook.com/resources to dive deeper:

☐ **Get the Workbook**
As mentioned on page 34 of Chapter 1, the companion guide to this book with exercises and prompts to help you apply the book's strategies to your business.

☐ **Listen to the Podcast: The New Talent Playbook**
Continue the conversation with Rob as he dives into topics like job descriptions, role clarity, and effective team structures—featuring subject matter experts, business owners, and solo insights.

☐ **Subscribe to Rob's Substack:** *The New Talent Playbook*
The talent landscape is constantly evolving. Don't get left behind. Get Rob's take on culture, hiring, leading in the face of AI, and more – all delivered straight to your inbox.

WORKBETTERNOW

Ready to unlock the nearshore talent advantage?

Scan to schedule a consultation with WorkBetterNow and start building your dream team!

Mention "New Talent Playbook" and get 150 USD off of the first three months of service.

ACKNOWLEDGEMENTS

To the WBN Certified Professionals™—You are the heartbeat of WBN. Every day, you bring skill, dedication, and heart to helping our clients achieve their missions. The work you do not only makes their businesses stronger, it changes the lives of their teams, customers, and communities. You inspire me daily.

To WBN clients—Thank you for trusting us with such an important part of your business. That trust means the world to me and our team. The fact that you've embraced our CPs, welcomed them into your teams, and empowered them to succeed is what makes this all work. Your openness and commitment to partnership have created stories of success I'm proud to share anywhere.

To the incredible WBN team—You've taken Andrew's and my vision and made it a reality. Your commitment, creativity, and willingness to jump in wherever needed are the reasons we've been able to grow, adapt, and have the impact we do. Special shout-outs to Jessica, who went from being my assistant to WBN's General Manager and continues to lead with excellence; Sergio, who keeps me on track every day; and Gaby, whose leadership in bringing my speaking engagements, webinars, and podcasts to life has amplified our message far and wide.

To Andrew "AC" Cohen—My friend for over 35 years and my partner in this adventure we call WBN. Of all the conversations we've had over the years, that one in a Portland bar in 2018 stands out—the moment we decided to start an offshore talent company. What a ride it's been since. You've been the steady hand guiding the day-to-day at WBN, allowing me to focus on what I do best while knowing the company is in the best possible hands. I'm grateful for your trust, your leadership, your friendship, and the countless laughs along the way. I couldn't ask for a better partner or a better friend.

To the subject matter experts who contributed to this book—Your willingness to share your expertise filled in the gaps and allowed readers to get the very best advice in areas beyond my own knowledge. This book is stronger because of you.

To Norm Brodsky—From the day you told me what I didn't want to hear about my idea for the New York Enterprise Report to catching a flaw in an early version of this book, you've always told me the truth I needed. You've guided me in more ways than you can imagine—professionally and personally—and your influence shows up in how I think, lead, and make decisions every day.

To Jack Daly—So much of what I "figured out" in business came from hearing you speak, reading your books, and spending time with you. The lessons on sales, culture, and life are now woven into how I do business. I'm grateful not just for the wisdom, but for the friendship.

To Dan Donnelly—You've been a mentor, collaborator, and friend. Your realistic positivity, adaptability, and ability to turn goals into reality have shaped how I approach business.

To the hundreds of business owners I've met in peer groups and beyond—You may never know how much I've learned from you. Your willingness to share experiences, challenges, and victories has helped shape my thinking more than you can imagine.

To the coaches and experts I've learned from over the years—As the owner of a media company serving business owners, I've been fortunate to meet and learn from an extraordinary range of people. Your insights have stayed with me and, in many ways, live inside these pages.

To Strategic Coach and Dan Sullivan—Your concepts have challenged me to think differently—and bigger. The impact on my business and my life has been profound, and I'm grateful to be part of that community.

To Steve Gordon and the Million Dollar Author team—Thank you for taking my notes, presentations, and interviews and helping me shape them into a book. This project wouldn't exist without your talent and guidance.

And finally, to my family—Maria, Mateo, and Carolina—You keep me inspired, grounded, and loved. Thank you for the sacrifices that come with life alongside an entrepreneur, for tolerating my crazy ideas, and for reminding me what truly matters. You may never know the full extent of the ways you inspire me, but I do.

ENDNOTES

1   Inc 5000 2024. Inc., www.inc.com/profile/workbetternow. Accessed 18 Sept. 2024.

2   "Number of Unemployed Persons per Job Opening, Seasonally Adjusted." Bls.gov, 2009, https://www.bls.gov/charts/job-openings-and-labor-turnover/unemp-per-job-opening.htm#. JOLTS Annual Story. 2009, www.bls.gov/opub/mlr/2009/05/art2full.pdf. Accessed 20 Sept. 2024.

3   "July 15, 2024 - ITR Economics." ITR Economics, 16 July 2024, itreconomics.com/portfolio/july-15-2024/. Accessed 20 Sept. 2024.

4   Maguire, Ed. "Momenta's Take: Generation Z." Momenta, 14 May 2024, www.momenta.one/insights/gen_z_enters_the_workforce. Accessed 20 Sept. 2024.

5   Bizjournals.com, 2024, https://www.bizjournals.com/buffalo/news/2024/01/28/hiring-managers-gen-z-workers-workplace-workforce.html. Accessed 20 Sept. 2024.

6   Robinson, Bryan. "Gen Z Careers the Worst to Manage, 45% of Hiring Managers Say." Forbes, 4 June 2024, https://www.forbes.com/sites/bryanrobinson/2024/05/26/gen-z-careers-the-worst-to-manage-45-of-hiring-managers-say/.

7   "'Lazy Girl Jobs' Are Trending in Rally against Burnout Culture." NBC News, 17 Aug. 2023, www.nbcnews.com/business/lazy-girl-jobs-burnout-culture-rcna97367. Accessed 20 Sept. 2024.

8   Liu, Jennifer. "The Lowest Salary Americans Will Accept at a New Job Reached a Record High." CNBC, CNBC, 17 Apr. 2024, https://www.cnbc.com/2024/04/17/salary-us-workers-expect-at-a-new-job-reaches-record-high.html. Accessed 20 Sept. 2024.

9   "How Much Does a Vacant Position Cost a Business?" 4 Corner Resources, 28 Feb. 2019, www.4cornerresources.com/blog/costs-of-vacant-position/. Accessed 20 Sept. 2024.

10   10 Ways to Engage Remote Workers. https://cloudtask.info/content-formats/articles/10-ways-to-engage-remote-workers/. Accessed 20 Sept. 2024.

11   "US Workers Would Take 20% Pay Cut for Better Quality of Life, Survey Finds." Voice of America, 1 Feb. 2024, www.voanews.com/a/us-workers-would-take-20-pay-cut-for-better-quality-of-life-survey-finds-/7463687.html. Accessed 20 Sept. 2024.

12   Boatman, Andrea. "13 Best Practices to Observe for Recruiting Top Talent." AIHR, 3 Sept. 2024, https://www.aihr.com/blog/recruiting-top-talent/ 21 Sept. 2024.

13   Cole, Kat. "New Hires and the First 40 Hours." Checking In with Kat Cole, 25 Apr. 2021, https://katcole.substack.com/p/growing-and-hiring. Accessed 21 Sept. 2024.

14   Anderson, Mae. "Almost All Small Businesses Are Using a Software Tool That Is Enabled by AI." AP News, 24 Sept. 2024. Accessed 24 Sept. 2024.

Made in the USA
Middletown, DE
16 November 2025